Migrating to

Office 95 & Office 97

A Corporate User's Quick Reference

Laura Monsen

Migrating to Office 95 and Office 97: A Corporate User's Quick Reference

Library of Congress Catalog No.: 97-80900

ISBN: 0-7897-1569-4

99 98   7 6 5 4 3 2 1

Interpretation of the printing code: the rightmost double-digit number is the year of the book's printing; the rightmost single-digit number, the number of the book's printing. For example, a printing code of 98-1 shows that the first printing of the book occurred in 1998.

Screen reproductions in this book were created using Collage Plus from Inner Media, Inc., Hollis, NH.

Contents at a Glance

Table of Contents

3 Upgrading to Microsoft Excel 95 and Excel 97   57

4 Upgrading to Microsoft Access 95 and Access 97   105

Credits

Publisher
John Pierce

Executive Editor
Jim Minatel

Director of Editorial Services
Carla Hall

Managing Editor
Thomas F. Hayes

Acquisitions Editor
Jill Byus

Development Editor
Rick Kughen

Production Editor
Heather E. Butler

Editors
Anne Owen, Tom Stevens

Technical Editor
Russ Jacobs

Book Designer
Ruth Harvey

Cover Designer
Dan Armstrong

Production Team
Nicole Ritch, Lisa Stumpf,
Scott Tullis

Indexer
Cheryl A. Jackson

Book Concept
Tom Ebeling

Composed in Stone Serif and Helvetica by Que Corporation.

About the Author

Laura Monsen is a professional instructor with more than seven years experience teaching computer application classes. For the past five years she has been teaching a variety of spreadsheet, project management, database, and graphic application classes for Productivity Point International (PPI), a leader in computer software training solutions. She teaches at the PPI site in San Antonio, Texas.

Laura is the author of *Using Microsoft Excel 97* recently published by Que. She has been a contributing author on several other Que computer reference books including *Special Edition Using Microsoft Project 98*, *Special Edition Using Microsoft PowerPoint 97*, and *Special Edition Using Microsoft Project 95*. Additionally, she frequently consults and tutors on Excel, Project, and PowerPoint. Laura has a B.A. in Economics from the University of the South, Sewanee, Tennessee.

ECCE QUAM BONUM

Acknowledgments

Jill Byus led the team of Que professionals who defined and edited this book. Her assistance and flexibility in its production allowed me to concentrate solely on writing. Jill was responsible for coordinating all the rest.

Another important person instrumental in developing this book who deserves my thanks is Rick Kughen. His superb editing suggestions ensured the text remained focused and concise. Go Packers!

Dedication

This book is dedicated to one of the most genuine people I've known, Rose Mayfield. Her infectious sense of humor and zest for life lives on, even though she is no longer with us.

We'd Like to Hear from You!

Que Corporation has a long-standing reputation for high-quality books and products. To ensure your continued satisfaction, we also understand the importance of customer service and support.

Tech Support

If you need assistance with the information in this book or with a CD/disk accompanying the book, please contact Macmillan Technical Support by phone at 317-581-3833 or via email at quecorp.com.

Orders, Catalogs, and Customer Service

To order other Que or Macmillan Computer Publishing books, catalogs, or products, please contact our Customer Service Department at 800/428-5331 or fax us at 800/882-8583 (International Fax: 317/228-4400). Or visit our online bookstore at http://www.mcp.com/.

Introduction

THIS BOOK IS DESIGNED AS A QUICK REFERENCE for people migrating to one of the newer versions of Microsoft Office—Microsoft Office 95 or Microsoft Office 97. Whether you are moving from Microsoft Office 4.3 (for Windows 3.1) or Microsoft Office 95, this book will help you get started.

You can purchase several different editions of Microsoft Office, including Professional Edition, Standard Edition, and Small Business Edition (Office 97 only). Each edition comes with a specific set of applications. This book focuses on the four most common applications—Word, Excel, Access, and PowerPoint.

Each application in Microsoft Office has its own version number. The table below lists the applications and their version numbers.

Application	Microsoft Office 4.3	Microsoft Office 95	Microsoft Office 97
Word	Word 6.0	Word 7.0	Word 8.0
Excel	Excel 5.0	Excel 7.0	Excel 8.0
Access	Access 2.0	Access 7.0	Access 8.0
PowerPoint	PowerPoint 4.0	PowerPoint 7.0	PowerPoint 8.0

Although the applications have version numbers, they are most often referred to by the Microsoft Office version they are part of rather than the application version. For example, Word 95 is used instead of Word 7.0. When referring to applications, this book will use the Microsoft Office version to avoid any possible confusion.

Who Should Use This Book?

This book is for the person who is currently using Microsoft Office and needs a guide to locate the commands and features that have been relocated or enhanced. The focus is on the differences between the Microsoft Office versions. As a quick reference guide, this book will outline where to find a command or feature. For detailed explanations and step-by-step instructions on using the Microsoft Office applications, there are several excellent series of books published by Que:

- ■ Using Series. Designed for the intermediate to advanced user, these books describe the most frequently used features in an application. *Using Microsoft Excel 97* is one of many books in this series.

- Special Edition Using Series. Designed for beginning to advanced user, these books describe each and every feature in an application. *Special Edition Using Microsoft Access 97* is one of many books in this series.

How This Book Is Organized

This book is divided into five sections. Within each section you will learn about new features in the application, how to convert files from previous versions of the application, and differences between each version. The sections are as follows:

- New and Enhanced Features, Common to All Programs. The emphasis in this section is on similar features available in all Microsoft Office applications. Learn about changes to the way you manipulate files, improved editing and drawing options, and the expanded online help in Microsoft Office.
- Upgrading to Word 95 and Word 97. The most important new features in Word are described in this section. Additionally, enhanced methods for creating and editing tables and templates, along with tracking document revisions is discussed.
- Upgrading to Excel 95 and Excel 97. This section describes the new editing and formatting options in Excel, the improved chart wizard, methods for sharing workbooks, and alternatives for importing and exporting data.
- Upgrading to Access 95 and Access 97. Highlights in this section include exploring the new database window; using wizards to create tables, queries, reports, and forms; and working in the Design View.
- Upgrading to PowerPoint 95 and PowerPoint 97. Chart animation, improved slide show techniques, and presentation alternatives are among the topics addressed in this section.

Conventions Used in This Book

Certain text formats and other conventions are used in *Migrating to Office 95 and Office 97* to help you use this book more easily. The following typefaces are used to distinguish specific text:

Typeface Conventions

Type Appearance	Meaning
bold	Examples of information that is typed. Also used to emphasize text.
italics	New terms or phrases when they are first defined. May also be used to emphasize text.
underlined characters	Indicates keyboard shortcuts for menu and dialog box commands.

Generally keys appear in this book just as they appear on the keyboard, such as Enter or Tab.

TIP Additional, helpful information that makes a procedure easier to perform or a feature easier to use is displayed in this format.

NOTE Additional, useful information is displayed in this format.

Throughout the topics covered in this book, you will see red numbers, like this **1** followed by a button name, field name, or description that corresponds with a figure that follows. Simply match the red number in the text with the same red number on a figure.

New and Enhanced Microsoft Office Features Common to All Programs

MICROSOFT OFFICE 95 AND OFFICE 97 possess many commands and features that are accessed and executed in the same way, regardless of the Office product you are using. This chapter introduces these new and enhanced features:

- **Managing Files.** Control the features of the Open dialog box, locate files quickly, and create new folders (directories) while saving files.

- **Editing and Drawing Enhancements.** AutoCorrect feature included in all programs.

- **Expanded Online Help.** Improved Table of Contents and Search Index interface, interactive help from the Answer Wizard and Office Assistant, and getting help from the Internet.

New Options When Opening Files

When you open files in Office 95 and Office 97, you will notice quite a change in the appearance of the Open dialog box. With one minor exception, the Office 95 and Office 97 dialog boxes are identical. The only difference is the Office 97 dialog box includes an icon to access the World Wide Web. The figures to the right show the Open dialog boxes for Office 4.3 (Figure 1.1) and Office 97 (Figure 1.2).

By default in Office 95 and Office 97, the files you create are stored in the My Documents folder. This enables you to quickly locate your files without having to remember which application you used to create the file. In Figure 1.1, several folders have been created and stored in separate files and by distinct categories.

Included in the Open dialog box in Figure 1.2 are a series of icons for locating files. You can **1** display the next level up in your list of folders (directories), **2** search the World Wide Web (available only in Office 97), **3** display a list of folders and files you frequently access (your "favorites"), and **4** add a folder or file to your list of "favorite" files.

Additionally, icons are available for changing the information you see regarding each folder or file. Your folders and files can be **5** displayed as a simple list of files, as **6** a list with detailed information about the files such as the name, size, type, and date the folder or file was last modified. You can also **7** display the Properties of a selected file, which includes information like Author, Date Created, Number of Pages, and Number of Revisions. With Word or PowerPoint files, you can **8** Preview the upper-left portion of the file in the preview window.

> **NOTE** In Excel, you must activate this property for each file you want to be able to preview; otherwise, a message appears in the preview window indicating "Preview Not Available." This feature is not available for Access databases.

The **9** Commands and Settings icon enables you to open a read-only copy of a file, sort your list of folders or files, and modify the properties of a file.

Another new feature of the Open dialog box is your ability to delete files directly from the Open dialog box. Deleted files are moved to the Recycle Bin in Office 95 and Office 97.

Converting files created in older versions of Microsoft Office will be addressed in the chapters devoted to each application (Word, Excel, Access, and PowerPoint).

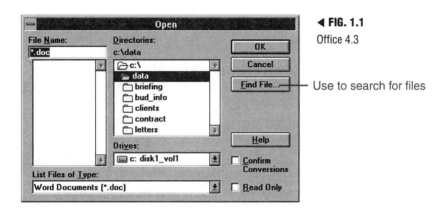

◀ FIG. 1.1

Office 4.3

Use to search for files

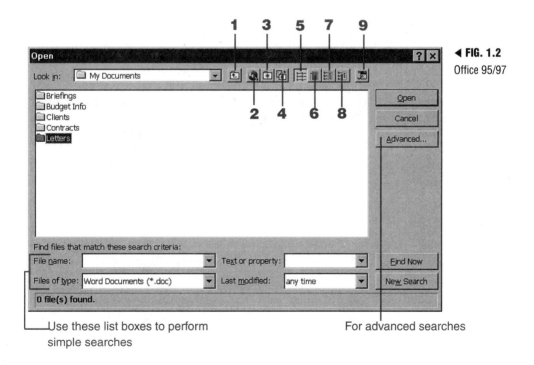

◀ FIG. 1.2

Office 95/97

Use these list boxes to perform simple searches

For advanced searches

Managing Files

Improved Methods for Locating Files

Finding files is typically done through the Open dialog box. In all versions of Microsoft Office, you can search for files based on file type, summary information (a.k.a. Properties), and the timeframe a file was created or last modified. In Office 95 and Office 97, the Open dialog box includes the capability to perform simple searches based on these options. You can also perform advanced searches by using the Advanced button in the Open dialog box.

Figure 1.3 shows the Advanced Search dialog box for Office 4.3. This dialog box consists of **1** three tabs used to define a search: Location, Summary, and Timestamp.

Figure 1.4 shows the Advanced Find dialog box for Office 97, which is accessed from the Open dialog box. The Office 95 and Office 97 Advanced Find dialog boxes are identical. The Office 95 and Office 97 Advanced Find dialog box has consolidated the search capabilities from three tabs of the Office 4.3 Advanced Search dialog box. Additionally, the Advanced Find dialog box now includes the capability to define multiple criteria in the search, and to use **2** more detailed properties in the search. Office 95 and Office 97 applications keep track of a number of unique properties for each file.

TIP **3** Include all subfolders for a more comprehensive search.

Figure 1.5 shows the Find All Files dialog box. In Windows 95, you can locate and open a file by using the Find feature. While there are several different ways to access the Find feature, one of the easiest is to click on the Start button and choose Find from the menu. You can then perform a **4** simple search using the three options tabs of the Find dialog box: Name & Location, Date Modified, and Advanced.

FIG. 1.3 ▶

Office 4.3—Advanced Search

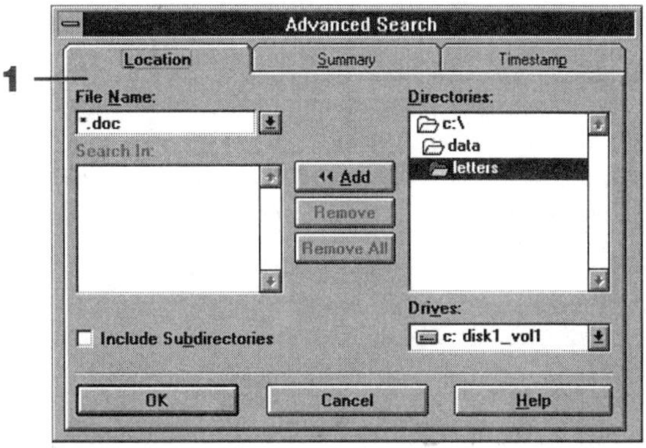

1

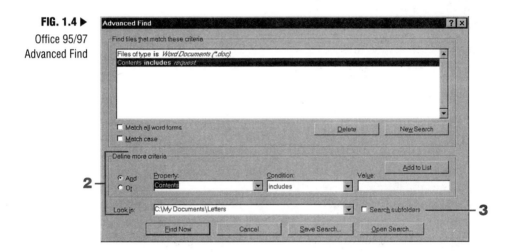

FIG. 1.4 ▶

Office 95/97
Advanced Find

2

3

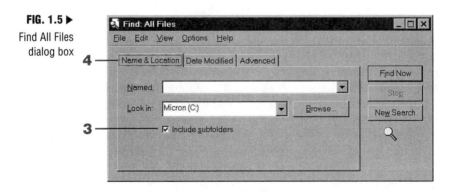

FIG. 1.5 ▶

Find All Files
dialog box

4

3

New Options in the Save As Dialog Box

You use the Save As dialog box to save a file for the first time, save a copy of the active file under another name, and save a copy of the active file in a different location.

When you save a file for the first time or select the File, Save As command, the Save As dialog box appears. You then indicate the filename, file type, and location where the file should be saved. Additionally, you have several options for protecting the file with a password. The figures to the right show the Save As dialog boxes for Office 4.3 (Figure 1.6) and Office 97 (Figure 1.7). The Office 95 and Office 97 Save As dialog boxes are identical.

In the Office 4.3 Save As dialog box, the default file location is the directory (folder) in which the program is stored. For example, the Winword directory would appear as the default file location for a Word 6.0 (Word 95) document.

When you save a new file in Office 95 and Office 97, the default file location, the My Documents folder, appears. If you choose the File, Save As command to make a copy of the file, the folder in which the original file is stored appears in the Save As dialog box.

When you save a file in Office 4.3, you generally give a file a name (and if necessary choose a file type), and then indicate the file location. In the revised Save As dialog box in Office 95 and Office 97, the location is selected first and then the filename and type.

Included in the Office 97 Save As dialog box is a series of icons for changing the location in which the file will be stored. You can **1** choose a different location to save the file in, **2** display the next level up in your list of folders (directories), or **3** display a list of folders and files you frequently access, also known as your "favorites."

> **NOTE** A new and very useful feature in the Office 95/97 Save As dialog box allows you to **4** create a new folder in which to store your file.

Your folders and files can be displayed as **5** a simple list of files, or as **6** a list with detailed information about the files such as the name, size, type, and date the folder or file was last modified. You can also **7** display the Properties of a selected file. The **8** Commands and Settings icon enables you to view the properties of a file, sort your list of folders or files, and map to a network drive. Just as in Office 4.3, the **9** Options button displays a list of choices for protecting your file.

Type in a filename

Use the Directories and Drives boxes to select the file location

FIG. 1.6 ▶
Office 4.3 Save As dialog box

If necessary, change the file type

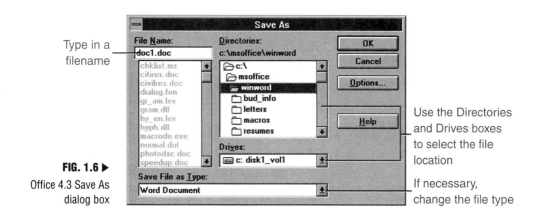

FIG. 1.7 ▶
Office 95/97 Save As dialog box

Choose the file location first

Type in a filename

If necessary, change the file type

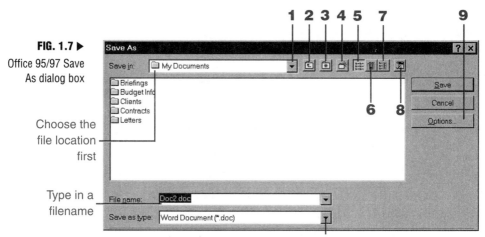

Editing and Drawing Enhancements

AutoCorrect Feature Is Now Available in All Office Programs

In Office 4.3, Microsoft Word is the only program that includes the AutoCorrect feature. While in Office 95 and Office 97, all programs contain this beneficial command. This feature automatically corrects words that users frequently mistype or misspell. New words have been added to the AutoCorrect list with each new version of Microsoft Office.

Additionally, AutoCorrect will correct any capitalization it perceives to be incorrect, such as capitalizing the first two letters of a word, failure to capitalize the first letter of a sentence, and so on.

AutoCorrect is also useful when you have a lengthy word or phrase you frequently type. You can add an abbreviation that corresponds to the word or phrase to AutoCorrect. When you type the abbreviation, AutoCorrect substitutes the complete word or phrase for the abbreviation. Following are a few examples:

Abbreviation	Complete Word or Phrase
ms	Microsoft
nc	North Carolina
afb	Air Force Base

NOTE   You find AutoCorrect under the Tools menu.

Figure 1.8 shows the AutoCorrect dialog box from Word 6.0, in Office 4.3.

FIG. 1.8 ▶

Office 4.3/Word
6.0 AutoCorrect
dialog box

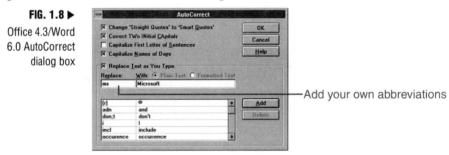

Add your own abbreviations

The features are virtually identical in the Word 7.0 (Office 95) AutoCorrect dialog box, shown in Figure 1.9. The other Office 95 programs have a dialog box similar to this one. Figure 1.10 shows the AutoCorrect dialog box in Excel 97. Figure 1.11 shows the Microsoft Word 97 AutoCorrect dialog box, which is slightly different from the other Office programs.

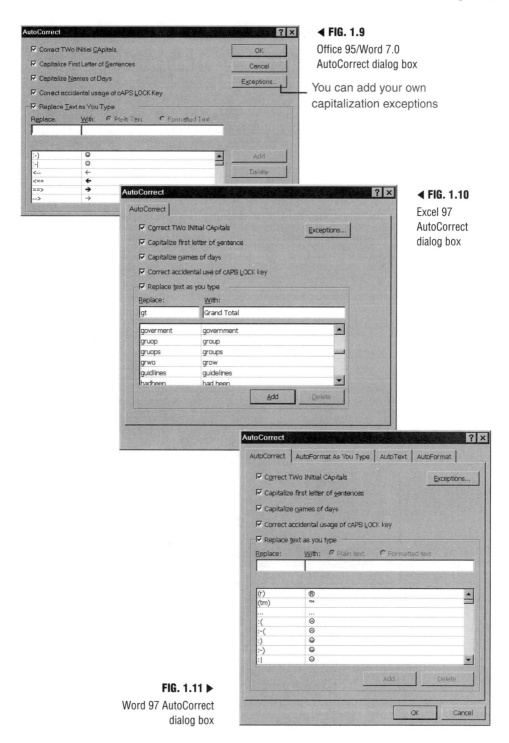

◀ FIG. 1.9

Office 95/Word 7.0
AutoCorrect dialog box

You can add your own
capitalization exceptions

◀ FIG. 1.10

Excel 97
AutoCorrect
dialog box

FIG. 1.11 ▶
Word 97 AutoCorrect
dialog box

Editing and Drawing Enhancements

Using Office Art (Office 97 Only)

An exciting new feature in all Office 97 programs is called Office Art. Expanding on the WordArt feature, you can now add WordArt, three-dimensional objects, and other shapes and drawn objects to your Office 97 files. WordArt is not available to other versions of Office.

To access this feature, simply display the Drawing toolbar in any program. Figure 1.12 shows the Drawing toolbar along with some of the objects you can add to your files. **1** WordArt has been integrated into this toolbar. Figures 1.13, 1.14, and 1.15 show some of the drawing options, including the **2** AutoShapes, **3** Shadow, and **4** 3-D effects you can apply to objects.

NOTE   Select the Drawing button on the Standard toolbar to display the Drawing toolbar.

FIG. 1.12 ▶

Objects created with the Drawing toolbar

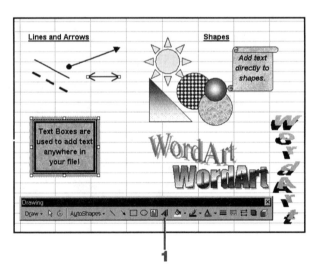

2 **3**

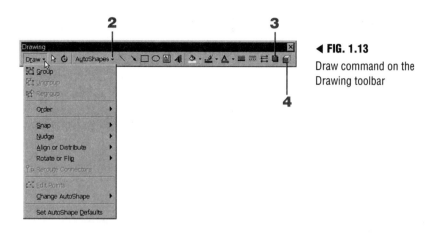

◀ **FIG. 1.13**

Draw command on the Drawing toolbar

4

FIG. 1.14 ▶

AutoShapes list

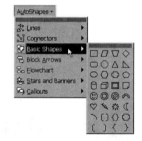

◀ **FIG. 1.15**

Apply Shadows

Expanded Online Help

Revised Table of Contents and Index Help Screens

With each new version of Office, Microsoft has improved the online help available to users. The Office 4.3 Help includes a general table of contents, as shown in Figure 1.16, and provides a search feature and index. The Office 95 and Office 97 Help Topics dialog boxes are similar. Included in the Help Topics dialog box are three tabs: Contents, Index, and Find.

Figure 1.17 shows an example of the Contents tab of the Excel 97 Help Topics dialog box. In Office 95 and Office 97, the table of contents has been revised to display a longer list of topics. Each general topic is represented by a **1** book icon. When you double-click on the book icon, a list of subtopics appears, and the symbol changes to an **2** open book icon. Specific help topics display a page icon with a **3** question mark (?), while additional subtopics display a book icon.

Figure 1.18 shows an example of the Index tab of the Excel 97 Help Topics dialog box. This feature is similar to the Search capability in Office 4.3. You enter the first few letters of the topic you need more information about, and a list of the corresponding help topics appears.

The third tab in the Help Topics dialog box accesses the Find feature. This feature enables you to locate all the help screens that contain a word or phrase in the help topic. The Find feature conducts a search of the text in the body of the help screens and displays a list of all help topics that contain the word or phrase for which you searched.

FIG. 1.16 ▶

Office 4.3 Help screen

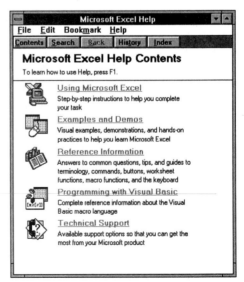

FIG. 1.17 ▶

Office 95/97 Help Topics—
Contents tab

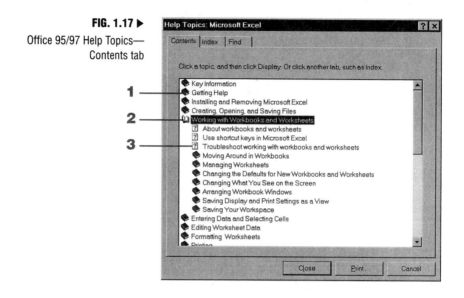

FIG. 1.18 ▶

Office 95/97 Help Topics—
Index tab

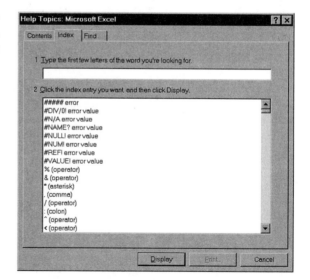

Expanded Online Help

Introducing the Answer Wizard and Office Assistant

In Office 95, a new feature has been added to the online help, making it easier to find information about your programs. This new help feature is the Answer Wizard, shown in Figure 1.19.

In step 1, you type in your question. Figure 1.19 shows how you can use the Answer Wizard to seek help with creating a database. In step 2, a list of topics relating to creating databases appears. Some of the help topics provide step-by-step procedures, and others display sample screens with interactive help.

Additionally, you continue to have the option of locating help topics through the Contents, Index, and Find tabs in the Help Topics dialog box.

In Office 97, the Answer Wizard has been replaced with the Office Assistant. The Office Assistant appears automatically when you first open an Office 97 program. At first you might be uncomfortable with the appearance of the Assistant; however, you will soon discover how useful it can be!

 You can resize or close the Office Assistant if you prefer not to receive assistance, or if the Office Assistant obstructs your viewing your files. To display the Office Assistant again, use the button on the toolbar or press F1.

The default image used for the Office Assistant is a paper clip called "Clippit" (see Figure 1.20). Use the **1** Options button in the Office Assistant pop-up to display a gallery of images you can use, including ones that look like Albert Einstein, William Shakespeare, a dog, a cat, a spacecraft, a bouncing dot, and earth.

> **NOTE**   Depending on how Office 97 was loaded on your machine, you may need the Office 97 CD to change the Office Assistant image.

FIG. 1.19 ▶

Office 95 Answer Wizard

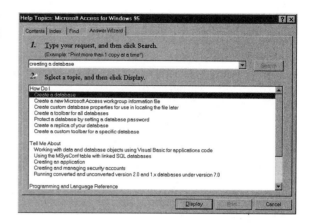

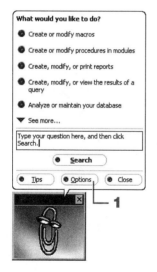

◀ FIG. 1.20

Office Assistant in Office 97

Expanded Online Help

Online Help via the Internet (Office 97 Only)

Microsoft has dedicated a large number of Web pages to provide additional information about its software programs. One of the most useful features in Office 97 is the capability to access this information directly from the Help menu. Figure 1.21 shows a typical Office 97 Help menu with the list of topics on which you can get help. The first few topics are always devoted to the program in which you are working. Figure 1.21 shows how you can get **1** free software, **2** information about upcoming changes or additions to the program, **3** answers to questions many users ask about the program, and **4** support from the Microsoft staff and power users of the software.

In addition, Microsoft provides Internet users with a **5** tutorial on using the Web, a list of the best Web sites, and a search capability.

Figure 1.22 shows the result of selecting Product News from the list of help topics.

NOTE   You must have access to the Internet and a Web browser program, such as Netscape Navigator or Internet Explorer, to use the Microsoft on the Web help.

FIG. 1.21 ▶

The Office 97 Help menu

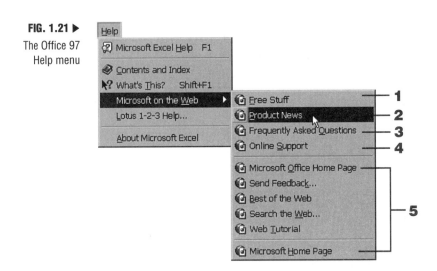

FIG. 1.22 ▶

An example of the
Product News
Web page for
Microsoft Excel

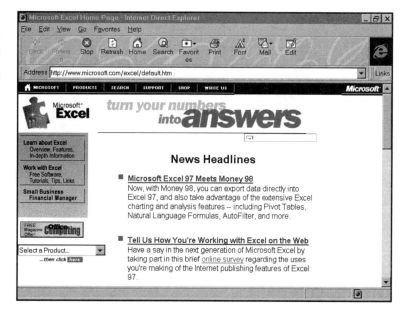

FIG. 1.22 ▶

An example of the
Product News
Web page for
Microsoft Excel

Upgrading to Microsoft Word 95 and Word 97

IF YOU ARE MIGRATING FROM Office 4.3 to Office 95 or Office 97, you will be pleased with the new and enhanced features that have been added to Word. The features introduced in this chapter are grouped by topic:

- **What's New.** Learn about the new features that have been added to Word.

- **Managing Files.** Convert the files you created in previous versions of Word to your current version of Word. Use the built-in templates to quickly create resumes, newsletters, legal pleadings, Web pages, brochures, memos, and awards. Save your Word files in HTML format so that they can be used as Web pages.

- **Editing Text.** Explore the revised spelling and grammar options.

- **Tables.** See how you can use the new Table and Border toolbars and the new Draw Table command to create and modify tables. Reformat the row height and column width.

- **Templates and Forms.** Discover the new built-in templates added to Word 95 and Word 97. Create your own custom templates.

- **Font Enhancements.** Improve your documents with the new font enhancements.

- **Tracking Revisions.** Tracking changes to a document has never been easier than with the new workgroup features.

Keep on top of *exactly* who made each change with the expanded revision marks. View comments added by colleagues. Merge several copies of a document into on document to see all changes and comments. Compare the original text to the revised text quickly.

What's New

Word 95

Word 95 contains a number of new or enhanced features. The following list describes many of these new features:

- **AutoFormat As You Type.** As you type, you can apply specific types of formatting to your document. You can format borders, headings, ordinal numbers, fractions, numbered lists, and bulleted lists. You activate this feature through the Tools, Option command. Select the AutoFormat tab in the Options dialog box to select from the list of formatting choices.

- **Editing Email.** If you use Microsoft Exchange/Schedule+ for email, you can use Word to create and edit email messages.

- **Highlighting Text.** Places a colored background behind text. Especially useful if you are sharing documents with colleagues and want to "flag" text you have changed. There is a new tool on the Formatting toolbar for highlighting text.

- **Templates.** Templates are now easier to locate and use. Three distinct styles have been created for templates: professional, contemporary, and elegant. Some templates use wizards to assist you in creating documents.

- **Tip Wizard.** This feature tracks your actions and makes suggestions on easier ways to accomplish the same action. The Tip Wizard is represented by a button with a lightbulb image on the Standard toolbar. Replaces Tip of the Day.

- **Spelling Indicator.** When you type in text that may be misspelled, a red wavy line appears under the word. This provides you with an immediate indication that Word does not recognize your text.

    NOTE   To see examples of the new features in Word 95, use the Answer Wizard. Type in **what's new** in the Answer Wizard search box and press Enter. Select What's New in Microsoft Word 95 from the list of help topics.

Word 97

Word 97 includes all the enhancements listed under the Word 95 section, as well as some additional features. The following list describes the most significant of these new features:

- **AutoComplete.** When you type in common entries (dates, names of the month or week, salutations and closings, mailing instructions), Word automatically displays the full text. You accept the text by pressing Enter. Choose <u>I</u>nsert, <u>A</u>utoText for a list of categories of common entries Word can complete. Select AutoTe<u>x</u>t to see an alphabetical list of all entries.

- **AutoSummarize.** The main points in a lengthy document are identified, and a summary is generated. Choose <u>T</u>ools, <u>A</u>utoSummarize to see a list of options you can choose from.

- **Formatting Additions.** Several new effects have been added to enhance text, including shadows, outlines, and engraving. You can also animate text so it blinks, shimmers, or sparkles. Borders can be added to the current page or every page in the document and are visible in the Page Layout view.

- **Internet and Intranet Features.** You can save your Word document in an HTML format (used for Web pages), apply color or texture to the background, use the new Online Layout view (which contains a feature called Document Map) to display the main components of a document, or create a *hyperlink* (a pointer) from one document to another, including Internet Web pages.

- **Table Enhancements.** You can draw a table and use the Table and Borders toolbar to quickly format it. This version of Word also enables you to evenly distribute the rows and columns in a table and change the orientation of the text.

- **Virus Alert.** Opening a file in Office 97 that contains a macro triggers an alert message warning you that the file contains a macro and that macros may contain viruses. Because most computer viruses are macros, this message is particularly useful when opening files from other users.

- **Versions.** Word 97 enables you to save versions of the document in the same file rather than saving each version as a separate document. This command is available under the <u>F</u>ile menu.

- **Visual Basic.** Replaces WordBasic for creating macros. Macros created in WordBasic can be converted to Visual Basic.

There are some additional enhancements and minor changes in Word 97:

- New templates and wizards are available.
- You can add shading to text and borders around paragraphs.
- There are more choices for formatting numbered and bulleted lists.
- The Find, Replace, and GoTo commands have been consolidated.
- The Tip Wizard has been removed in favor of the Office Assistant.

> **NOTE** Some features from previous versions have been renamed, and some of the commands have been moved to other menus in Word 97. See a list at the end of this chapter for command menu changes.

Exchanging Files Between Different Versions of Word

You can display a file created in an earlier version of Word by simply opening the file in your current version of Word. For example, if you have a file created in Word 6.0 and you are currently using Word 97, open the Word 6.0 file in Word 97 to display it.

To convert a file from an earlier version of Word to a newer version, you must save the file. If you are using Word 95, when you save the file, it is immediately converted into a Word 95 format. In Word 97, when you attempt to save a file created in an earlier version of Word, the dialog box displayed in Figure 2.1 appears. You have the choice of saving the file as a Word 97 file or keeping it as a Word 6.0/95 file.

When you create a file in Word 95, you do not have to save the file in a Word 6.0 format to open the file in Word 6.0. Any formatting features in Word 95, such as highlighting text, will not be displayed in Word 6.0. If the file is changed in Word 6.0, any formatting features specific to Word 95 will be lost.

When you create a file in Word 97, you must save the file in a Word 6.0/95 format if you want to open the file in these versions of Word. Figure 2.2 shows an example of a Word 97 file being saved in a Word 6.0/95 format. Any formatting features specific to Word 97 will not be saved with the file.

When Word 97 was first released, documents saved in a Word 6.0/95 format were saved as Rich Text Format (.rtf) files. Additionally, users were noticing a significant increase in file size when they saved Word 97 files into Word 6.0/95 format, due to the compression features in Word 97. Today, Microsoft's Web site contains a revised converter file that fixes these problems.

To download this converter, you must have access to the Internet. In Word 97, choose Help, Microsoft on the Web, and select Free Stuff. When the Microsoft Free Stuff screen appears, scroll down in the list until you see **Word 6.0/95 Binary Converter for Word 97**, as shown in Figure 2.3. Choose the **1** More Info link to see an explanation of what this converter will do.

> **TIP** Ask the Office Assistant how to convert several files to Word 97 at one time.

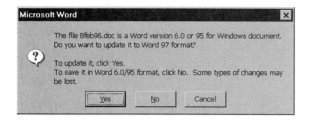

◀ **FIG. 2.1**
Word 97 update dialog box

FIG. 2.2 ▶
Word 97 Save As
dialog box

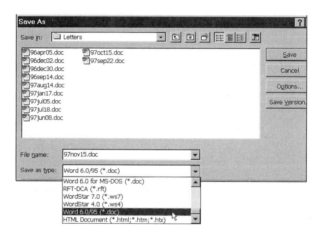

FIG. 2.3 ▶
Download the
Word 6.0/95
Converter

1

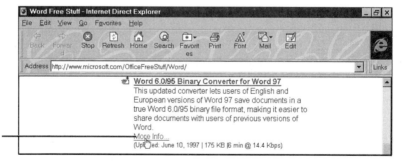

Managing Files

Creating New Files Using the Built-in Templates

When you choose the File, New command in Word 95 and Word 97, you discover a wide range of built-in templates that hardly resemble the templates found in Word 6.0. The former templates have been updated to depict professional, contemporary, and elegant styles. Many of the new templates use wizards, which prompt you for information in order to create the document.

As you can see in Figures 2.4 and 2.5, the templates are now divided into distinct categories, making it much easier to locate templates more quickly.

Figure 2.4 shows the New dialog box in Word 95. The Award Wizard template on the Other Documents tab has been selected. A preview of the document appears on the right side of the dialog box.

Figure 2.5 shows the New dialog box in Word 97. The Contemporary Report has been selected from the Reports tab, and a preview of the report appears on the right side of the dialog box. One of the tabs in this figure lists the Office 95 templates. This tab appears only if Word 95 was on your machine when Word 97 was installed.

Many of the templates can be previewed, allowing you to see an overall depiction of the document before you create it. However, a few templates cannot be previewed, most notably the Web Pages templates.

> **NOTE** If you use the New button on the Standard toolbar to create a new document, the Blank Document template is automatically used to create the file. You must use the File, New command to see a list of the built-in templates.

> **TIP** If you have access to the Internet, you can use the Help, Microsoft on the Web, Free Stuff command to look for additional templates available from Microsoft.

FIG. 2.4 ▶

Word 95 New
dialog box

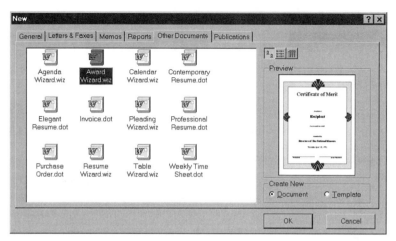

◀ FIG. 2.5

Word 97 New
dialog box

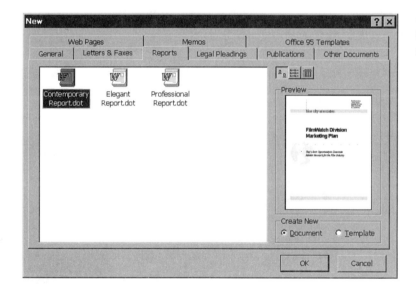

Saving Files in HTML Format (Word 97 Only)

You can save Word 97 files in the *Hypertext Markup Language (HTML)* format. This format is required for files that will be Web pages on the Internet World Wide Web or on your company's internal intranet. To save a file in the HTML format, choose File, Save as HTML.

As with other files, you need to supply a **1** location and **2** name for this file. Figure 2.6 shows an example of the Save As HTML dialog box. As part of the process to convert the Word file into HTML format, several dialog boxes may appear. Figure 2.7 shows one of the dialog boxes you may see. It warns you to save the file before converting to HTML because some formats may be lost as a result of the conversion.

Because Microsoft periodically makes new Web page authoring tools available, you may be asked if you want to connect to the Internet to check to see whether there is a new version of the Web page authoring tools. This will be followed by a prompt asking whether you want to access the Microsoft Web site to download a new version of these tools. Figures 2.8 and 2.9 show examples of these prompts.

Figure 2.10 displays the Microsoft Web page that provides a **3** status of the latest Web page authoring tools for Word 97.

After a Word 97 file has been converted to HTML, it appears differently on the screen. The toolbar buttons and menu commands are changed to provide tools to format and edit the HTML file.

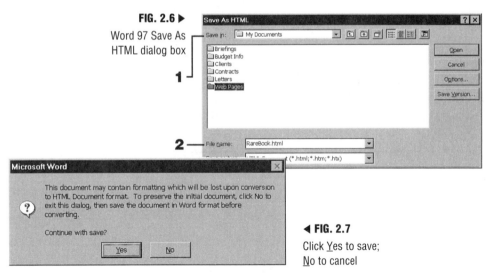

FIG. 2.6 ▶
Word 97 Save As HTML dialog box

◄ FIG. 2.7
Click Yes to save; No to cancel

◀ FIG. 2.8
Downloading
Web page
authoring tools

FIG. 2.9 ▶
Word 97
AutoUpdate

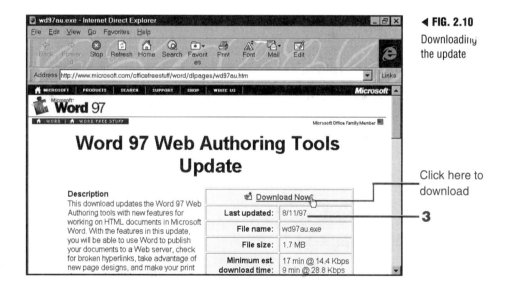

◀ FIG. 2.10
Downloading
the update

Click here to
download

3

Editing Text
Improved Spell Check and Grammar Options

Several significant additions have been made in the area of spelling and grammar in Word 95 and Word 97. When you type a word the program does not recognize, a red wavy line appears beneath the word. This provides you with an immediate indication that the word is located in the Microsoft Office or custom dictionaries. The word may be misspelled, a duplicate, an abbreviation, a proper name, or from a language other than English.

Additionally, Word 97 displays a wavy green line to alert you of a possible grammatical error.

In Word 6.0 and Word 95, the commands that check spelling and grammar are activated separately. As you can see in Figures 2.11 and 2.12, there is little difference in the options available in the Spelling dialog boxes of Word 6.0 and Word 95.

In Word 97, these two features have been combined into one command. Figure 2.13 shows the Spelling and Grammar dialog box in Word 97. You can set the parameters for spelling and grammar by selecting the **1** Spelling and Grammar tab in the Tools, Options dialog box, as shown on the left side of Figure 2.14 on the next page. The right side of this figure shows the grammar options you can select by clicking the **2** Settings button in the Options dialog box. You can also access the Options dialog box by choosing the Options button in the Spelling and Grammar dialog box.

In all versions of Word, the spelling and grammar commands are located under the Tools menu.

◄ FIG. 2.11

Word 6.0 Spelling dialog box

FIG. 2.12 ►

Word 95 Spelling dialog box

FIG. 2.13 ▶
Word 97 Spelling
and Grammar
dialog box

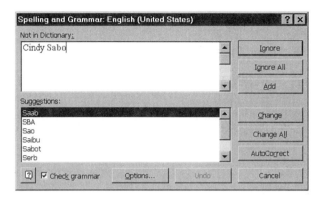

◀ FIG. 2.14
Spelling and
grammar options

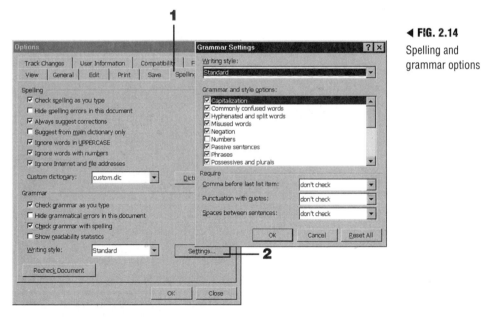

Table and Border Toolbars

In Word 6.0 and Word 95, a button on the Formatting toolbar activates the Borders toolbar, which is useful in applying borders to tables. Figure 2.15 shows a table in Word 6.0 with the Borders toolbar displayed below the table. On the Formatting toolbar, the mouse is pointing to the button that activates the Borders toolbar.

In Word 97, the new Tables and Borders toolbar has been added to the list of toolbars. This new toolbar includes the border features found on the Borders toolbar from Word 6.0 and Word 95 and adds common table features as well. Figure 2.16 on the next page shows a table in Word 97 with the Tables and Borders toolbar displayed below the table. On the Standard toolbar, the mouse is pointing to the button that activates this toolbar. Some of the commands available on the Tables and Borders toolbar are

- **1** Draw Table and Eraser
- **2** Line and Border Formats
- **3** Merge or Split Cells
- **4** Vertical Alignment
- **5** Distribute Rows or Columns Evenly
- **6** Table AutoFormat
- **7** Change Text Direction
- **8** Sort Ascending or Descending
- **9** AutoSum

FIG. 2.15 ▶
A Word 6.0 table

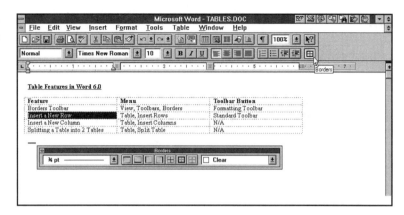

FIG. 2.16 ▶
A Word 97 table

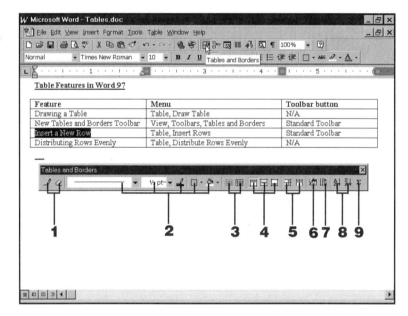

Tables

Drawing a Table (Word 97 Only)

In Word 97, you can create and format a table quickly by using the new Table, Draw Table command. By activating the new Tables and Borders toolbar, most of the table formatting options are within easy access.

NOTE   If you are not in the Page Layout view when you select the Draw Table command, a message appears asking whether you want to change to the Page Layout view.

The mouse pointer changes to the shape of a **1** pencil. Figure 2.17 shows the Page Layout view with the Tables and Borders toolbar.

Select the line style, weight, and color from the Tables and Borders toolbar and draw a rectangle for the outside border of the table. To create rows and columns in the table, **2** draw the horizontal and vertical lines exactly where you want them.

NOTE   You can use the Split Cells button to specify the rows and columns; however, this option spaces the rows and columns equally and uses the border style, weight, and color for the lines dividing the rows and columns.

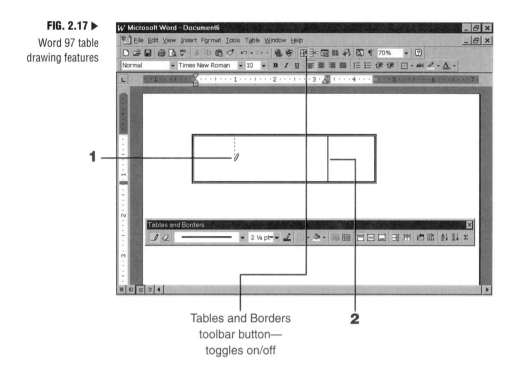

Tables and Borders
toolbar button—
toggles on/off

Distributing Rows and Columns Evenly in a Table (Word 97 Only)

A new feature in Word 97 is the capability to evenly space the rows and columns in a table. Formatting columns to have the same width or rows to have the same height can save time when you are trying to establish a uniform look to your tables.

NOTE   You can access the Distribute Columns Evenly and Distribute Rows Evenly commands from the new Tables and Borders toolbar or from the Tables menu.

Figure 2.18 shows a table before and after the Distribute Rows Evenly feature is used. The **1** Distribute Columns Evenly feature is also available on the Tables and Borders toolbar.

The text has also been centered vertically using the **2** center button on this toolbar.

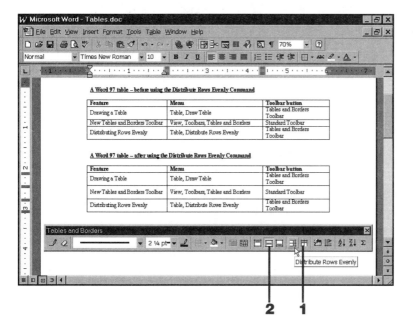

Changing Text Orientation in a Table (Word 97 Only)

A new feature in Word 97 is the capability to change the orientation of the text in a table. This feature has three settings: normal (left to right), top to bottom, and bottom to top. Each time you select the Change Text Direction command, it cycles through these three settings.

Figure 2.19 shows a table illustrating these three settings. The text in the middle of the table is selected. Notice the **1** Change Text Direction button on the Tables and Borders toolbar. The button image changes depending on the orientation of the selected text. Because the selected text is currently oriented top to bottom, the next direction available is bottom to top, as depicted on the button image.

Notice the **2** tools on the Formatting toolbar. Because the direction of the selected text is top to bottom, the orientation of many of the buttons has changed as well, including

- Left, Center, Right, and Justify Alignment
- Numbered and Bulleted Lists
- Decrease and Increase Indent

NOTE You can access the Text Direction command either from the Format menu or through a button on the Tables and Borders toolbar. Your cursor must be inside a table for this feature to be active.

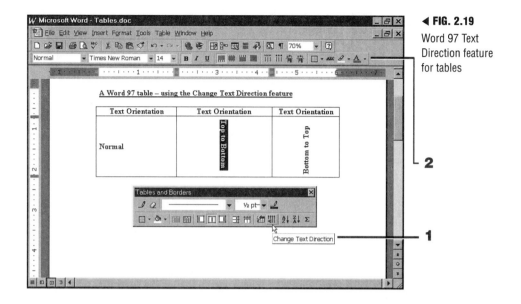

Word 97 Text
Direction feature
for tables

Templates and Forms

Using the Built-in Templates

Many of the templates in Word 95 and Word 97 are now designed with wizards to assist you in using the template. The wizards provide you with a list of choices for creating a document. To access the built-in templates, you must use the File, New command. Using the New button on the Standard toolbar immediately creates a blank document.

Figure 2.20 shows the New dialog box for Word 95. The list of templates is divided into categories, with **1** each category on a different tab. The Resume Wizard template on the Other Documents tab is selected. A **2** preview of the document created by a template appears on the right.

Figure 2.21 shows the first step in the Resume Wizard, asking which type of resume is to be created. A common feature of wizards is to provide an explanation or description of the selected item. In this example, the Functional resume has been created and an **3** explanation of who will benefit from this type of resume appears below the choices.

The New dialog box in Word 97 provides some **4** additional template categories, as you can see in Figure 2.22. Here, the Newsletter Wizard has been selected from the Publications tab. If you are upgrading from Office 95, the **5** templates available in Office 95 will appear on their own tab.

As you can see in Figure 2.23, the appearance of the wizards has been enhanced in Word 97. The diagram on the left of the screen depicts a **6** "road map" where you can enter the wizard at any step along the way.

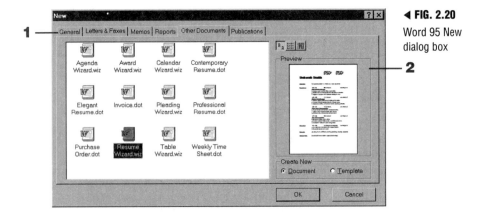

◀ **FIG. 2.20**

Word 95 New dialog box

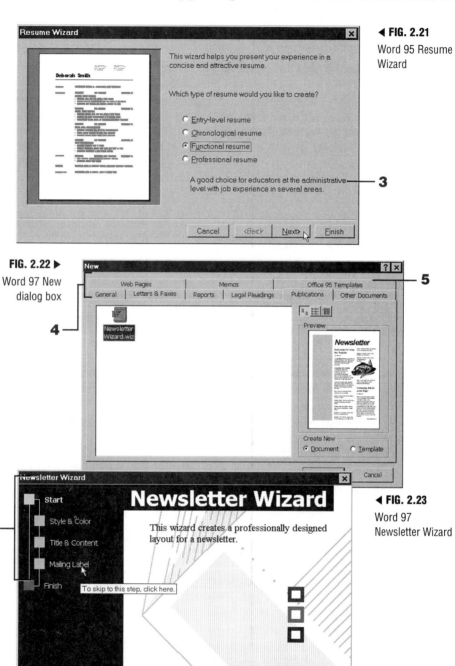

◀ **FIG. 2.21**
Word 95 Resume
Wizard

3

FIG. 2.22 ▶
Word 97 New
dialog box

5

4

◀ **FIG. 2.23**
Word 97
Newsletter Wizard

6

Templates and Forms

Creating Custom Templates

There are three ways to create your own templates in Word: create a template from "scratch," create a template based on an existing Word document, or create a template based on an existing template. Word 6.0 (Office 4.3) enables you to create templates by using the first two methods. With the templates that are now built in to Word 95 and Word 97, it is much easier to create custom templates based on these existing professionally designed templates.

If you create a template from scratch, or base a new template on an existing document, make sure that it is the active document in Word. To create a new template based on an existing template, choose File, New and select the template you want. If the template is a wizard, proceed through the wizard to create the document. Modify the document as necessary.

After the file is created, use the File, Save As command to save it as a template file. Figure 2.24 shows the Word 97 Save As dialog box, which is nearly identical to the Word 95 Save As dialog box. In the **1** Save As Type box, choose Document Template (*.dot). Word will automatically display the Templates folder in the **2** Save In box. The folder in which you save the template determines the tab in the New dialog box, shown in Figure 2.25, where you will find the template for future use. Templates saved directly in the Templates folder in the Save As dialog box (Figure 2.24) appear on the General tab of the New dialog box (Figure 2.25). If you save a template in a subfolder of the Templates folder, such as Memos or Web Pages, the template will appear on this tab in the New dialog box. In Figure 2.24, the template named Marketing Letter is being saved in the **3** Letters & Faxes subfolder. When a new document is created using the File, New command, the New dialog box, shown in Figure 2.25, displays a list of template tabs. The template Marketing Letter is selected on the Letters & Faxes tab in Figure 2.25.

> **TIP** To learn more about creating templates, use the online help. Look up information by typing **creating templates** in the Answer Wizard in Word 95 or the Office Assistant in Word 97.

FIG. 2.24 ▶
Word 97 Save As
dialog box

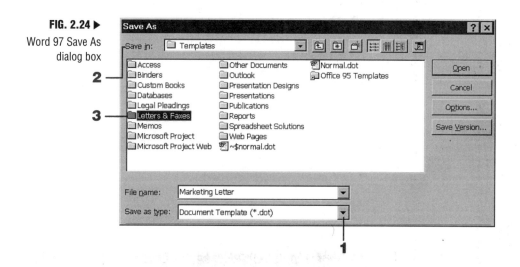

◀ FIG. 2.25
Word 97 New
dialog box

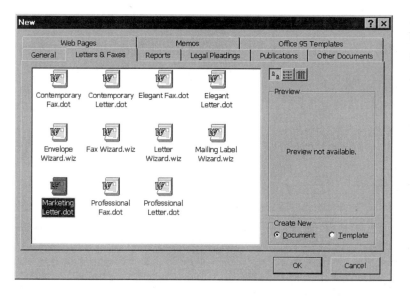

Font Enhancements

New Font Effects (Word 97 Only)

In all versions of Word, you have the ability to apply effects to your text. Among the most common are strikethrough (~~abc~~), subscript (H_2O), and all caps (ABC). Several new font effects have been included in Word 97.

These new font effects are illustrated in Figure 2.26. The new effects are **1** double strikethrough, **2** shadow, **3** outline, **4** emboss, and **5** engrave.

To access the effects, choose Format, Font. The Font dialog box, as shown in Figure 2.26, appears. The effects are located in the middle of the first tab of this dialog box. Use the **6** preview window at the bottom of the dialog box to see how the effect will impact the appearance of your text.

1 —— Double Strikethrough

2 —— Shadow

3 —— Outline

4 —— Emboss

5 —— Engrave

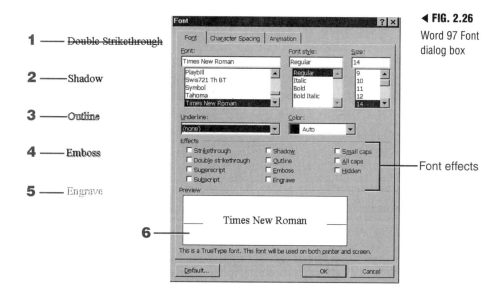

Word 97 Font
dialog box

Font effects

6

Font Enhancements

Applying Font Animation (Word 97 Only)

Office 97 contains many intranet and Internet features, one of which is the capability to create documents that can be viewed online. Word 97 includes a new enhancement, which will animate text in online documents. These font effects are not available to Office 4.x and Office 95 users.

You can access these new font effects through the Font dialog box. Choose Format, Font to display this dialog box. In the Font dialog box, select the **1** Animation tab (see Figure 2.27). The new effects are listed here:

- Blinking Background
- Las Vegas Lights
- Marching Black Ants
- Marching Red Ants
- Shimmer
- Sparkle Text

Use the **2** preview window at the bottom of the dialog box to see the how the animation will impact the appearance of your text.

> **NOTE** These animation effects appear only when the document is being viewed; they do not appear when the document is printed.

FIG. 2.27 ▶

The Animation tab
of the Font dialog
box in Word 97

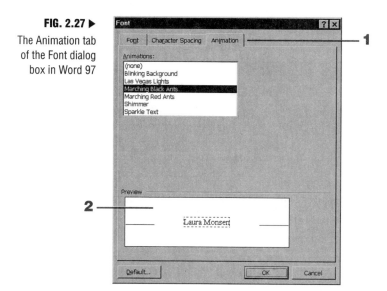

Tracking Revisions

Expanded Revision Marks (Word 97 Only)

All versions of Word (4.x, 95, and 97) include an option to color code changes made to a document by other users. Additionally, **1** a vertical marker appears in the left margin to flag the line changes made, which makes it quicker to locate each change.

Word 97 expands on this feature by adding **2** a pop-up note with the user's name and the date of the change, as you can see in Figure 2.28.

The users making changes must take several steps to ensure that you can see the changes they have made:

- Open the document to be changed.
- Select Tools, Track Changes, Highlight Changes. From the Highlight Changes dialog box (see Figure 2.29), select **3** Track Changes While Editing.

> **NOTE**   In Word 6.0 (Office 4.3) and Word 95, users should choose the Tools, Revisions command and activate the Mark Revisions While Editing option (see Figure 2.30) to display the color coded changes.

- Select Tools, Options. On the **4** User Information tab of the Options dialog box (see Figure 2.31), make sure the name of the person making the changes appears in the **5** Name box. This step is identical, regardless of the version of Word you are using.
- Make the necessary changes.

> **NOTE**   The Track Changes While Editing feature is active only for the current document. Each time you want to show the revision marks, you will have to activate this feature.

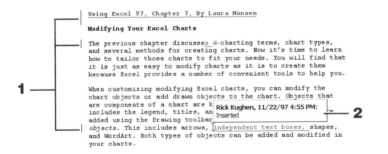

◀ **FIG. 2.28**

Word 97 enhanced revision marks

FIG. 2.29 ▶

Word 97
Highlight
Changes dialog
box

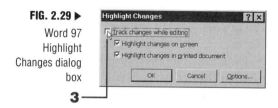

3

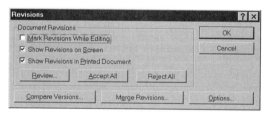

◀ FIG. 2.30

Word 6.0/95
Revisions dialog
box

FIG. 2.31 ▶

Word 97 User
Information tab

4

5

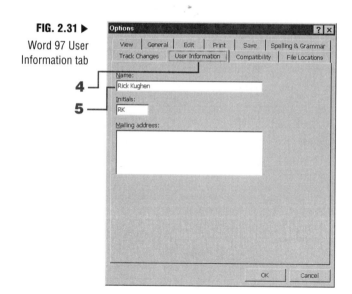

Adding Comments (Word 97 Only)

In Word 6.0 (Office 4.x) and Word 95, the Annotation command is used to insert notes into documents when reviewing the text. Figure 2.32 shows an example of annotations added into a Word 6.0 document. You add and view annotations in Word 95 the same way they are added in Word 6.0.

In Word 97, this command is now called Comment. To add a comment to a document, select the text the comment will pertain to and choose Insert, Comment. Figure 2.33 shows an example of a document with several comments added. Text referred to in the comment will be **1** highlighted in pale yellow, and the **2** comments view will appear in the lower portion of the screen. The **3** initials of each person who has added comments will appear in the comments view.

In Word 97, several new features have been added to comments. The text in the document will remain highlighted in pale yellow, even when the comments view is closed. To read a comment, simply position the mouse pointer over a piece of text. The highlight will turn dark yellow, and **4** the comment will pop up on the screen.

To display the comments view again, choose View, Comments.

> **TIP** There is a new toolbar in Word 97 designed to assist in inserting and reviewing changes made to documents. Choose View, Toolbars and select Reviewing to display this toolbar. Hovering the mouse over each of the buttons will make a ScreenTip appear, describing what each button does.

FIG. 2.32 ►

Annotations
added to a Word
6.0/95 document

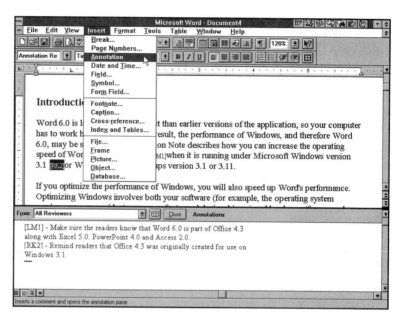

◄ FIG. 2.33

Comments added
to a Word 97 doc-
ument

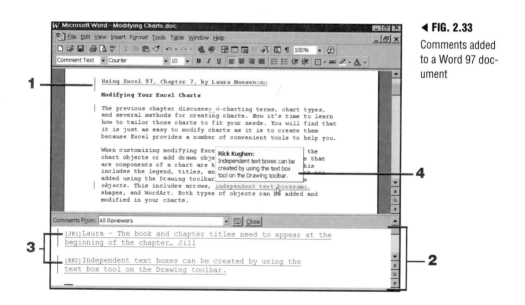

Tracking Revisions

Merging Documents (Word 97 Only)

A new and powerful feature in Word 97 is the capability to merge several copies of a document that have been reviewed and modified by different people. All the comments and revision changes from each copy are merged into one document.

NOTE This feature is not available in Word 6.0 or Word 95.

You can easily identify the revisions because Word underlines and changes the text color of all revisions and highlights comments. Position your mouse pointer next to the underlined or highlighted words, and a pop-up displays the name of the person making the change, the date the change was made, and what type of change was made.

To merge documents you must first open one of the documents (perhaps the original), and then choose Tools, Merge Documents. The Select File to Merge Into Current Document dialog box appears, as shown in Figure 2.34. Identify the file with which you want to merge the current file.

If you need to merge several files into the current file, repeat the Merge Documents command until all files have been merged. If several people have edited the same word or phrase, all edits are shown together so you can decide which one to accept.

FIG. 2.34 ▶

Word 97 merge
feature

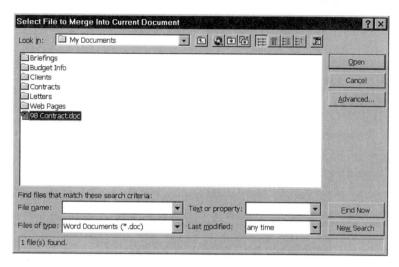

Tracking Revisions

Reviewing Document Changes

When revisions are made to a Word document, in any version, the changes are color coded to indicate who made the changes. An enhancement has been added to Word 97 when you are tracking revisions or edits made by others to documents. You can quickly alternate between three settings:

- View the changes with highlighting (underlines and color)
- View the changes without highlighting
- View the original text, without the changes

This enables you to look at the changes proposed by others, see the changes implemented (deleted text removed), and compare the changes to the original text.

Figure 2.35 shows the Review Revisions dialog box in Word 95. The comparable dialog box in Word 97, the Accept or Reject Changes dialog box, appears in Figure 2.36.

NOTE In both Word 95 and Word 97, these dialog boxes will remain on the screen as you scroll around the document, edit data, change views, and even display other documents.

FIG. 2.35 ▶
Word 95

A new feature in Word 97

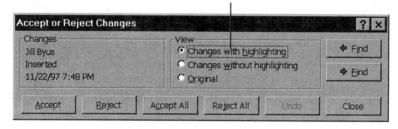

◀ FIG. 2.36
Word 97

Saving Document Versions (Word 97 Only)

In Word 6.0 (Office 4.3) and Word 95, keeping different versions of a document requires you to save each version as a separate file. In Word 97, you can save different versions of a document within the same file. To distinguish one version from another, Word prompts you to add a comment to each version.

To save a version of a document, choose File, Versions. The Versions In dialog box appears, as shown in Figure 2.37. Choose the Save Now button, and the Save Version dialog box appears (see Figure 2.38). Type in any comments that will help distinguish this version from other versions.

To open a version, choose File, Versions and select the version you want to open.

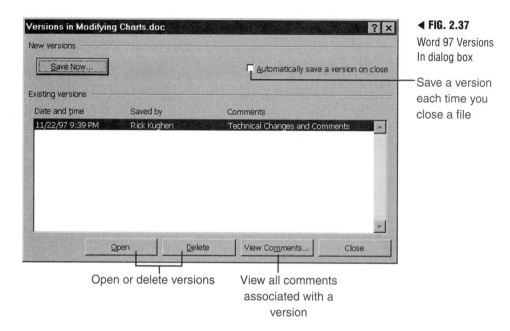

Word 97 Versions
In dialog box

Save a version
each time you
close a file

Open or delete versions

View all comments
associated with a
version

FIG. 2.38 ►
Word 97 Save
Version dialog
box

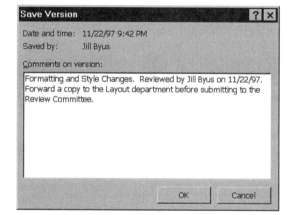

3

Upgrading to Microsoft Excel 95 and Excel 97

IF YOU ARE MIGRATING FROM Office 4.3 to Office 95 or Office 97, you will be pleased with the new and enhanced features that have been added to Excel. Some of the features introduced in this chapter are

- **Managing Files.** Convert files created in previous versions of Excel to your current version of Excel. Save your Excel files in HTML format so they can be used as Web pages.
- **Editing and Formatting.** See how to merge several cells into one cell. Use the AutoComplete feature to expedite data entry. Apply different formats to cells based on the type of data in the cell.
- **Formulas and Functions.** Create functions more easily with the enhanced Paste Function option.
- **Charts and Maps.** Create regional and global maps using data in your worksheets. Explore the enhanced Chart Wizard, which includes new chart types and options.
- **Workgroup Features.** Allow other members of your workgroup to simultaneously access your workbooks to insert comments or make editing changes.
- **Importing and Exporting Data.** Convert Excel lists into Access tables and quickly create input forms or reports based on the worksheet data. Use the Microsoft Query program to import data from databases into an Excel worksheet.

The following list identifies each version of Excel and the Microsoft Office version with which it is associated. Excel 95 and Excel 97 will be used when referring to those versions.

Excel Version Number	Microsoft Office Version
Excel 5.0	Office 4.3
Excel 7.0 (often referred to as Excel 95)	Office 95
Excel 8.0 (often referred to as Excel 97)	Office 97

What's New

Excel 95

The following list describes many of the new or enhanced features in Excel 95:

■ **Sharing Lists.** Share workbooks with other users and track the changes made to the workbook. You can enter or sort data, or add rows or columns, but you cannot change cell formatting or modify formulas.

■ **Converting Excel Data into Access Tables.** Convert Excel lists into Access tables and quickly create input forms or reports based on the data, all from within Excel.

■ **Microsoft Excel Viewer.** Similar to the Viewer in PowerPoint, users who do not have Excel can open and view Excel files you send to them.

■ **Plotting Maps.** Worksheet data organized geographically can be plotted on a map, with color coding distinguishing the different data.

■ **Built-in Templates.** Templates provide predesigned worksheet forms such as a purchase order, invoice, and expense statement. Data entered into a form can be stored in lists or databases. You can create templates that store data in lists or databases by using the new Template Wizard with Data Tracking.

Additional enhancements and minor changes in Excel 95 include the following:

■ Move a range of cells from one workbook or worksheet to another by dragging the border of the selected cells.

■ Notes added to cells automatically display when you place the mouse pointer on a cell.

■ What's This help, represented by a question mark, is available in all dialog boxes and provides more information on the items in a dialog box.

■ As you enter text in a list, Excel compares the characters you are typing with other entries in the same column and completes the entry for you.

Excel 97

Excel 97 includes all the enhancements listed for Excel 95, as well as some additional features. The following list describes the most significant of these new features:

■ **Chart Wizard.** Creating charts has never been easier than with the improved Chart Wizard in Excel 97. Several new chart types are available, along with added features such as data tables and screen tips identifying each part of a chart.

- **Editing and Data Entry Enhancements.** Excel 97 allows you to undo multiple actions. You can apply conditional formats to cells and validate data as it is entered into a cell.

- **Internet and intranet Features.** You can save your Excel document in an HTML format (used for Web pages). Create a *hyperlink*, a pointer, from one document to another including Internet Web pages. Access useful information online from Microsoft through the Help menu.

- **Retrieve Data from External Databases.** Use Microsoft Query and the new Query Wizard to set up a data source, connect to a database, select data to retrieve, and even sort or filter the data before bringing it into Excel.

- **Sharing Workbooks.** One person can edit one worksheet in a workbook while someone else can edit another worksheet simultaneously. When one user saves the workbook, the other users who share it see the changes made by that user. Different people can access adjacent data in the same worksheet. The shared workbook feature replaces the shared list feature in Microsoft Excel 95.

- **Workgroup Features.** You can merge copies of a workbook to consolidate comments and editing changes. A new toolbar, the Comments and Review toolbar, enables you to quickly view all comments made to a shared workbook. The Microsoft Binder lets you group documents from different programs into a single place for editing and review.

- **Worksheet Function Changes.** The Paste Function command replaces the Function Wizard. You can collapse (and expand) a dialog box to select cell ranges in your worksheets while using a function. Additional worksheet functions have been added to Excel.

Following are some additional enhancements and minor changes in Excel 97:

- The maximum number of worksheet rows has increased from 16,384 to 65,536.

- The default number of worksheets in a new workbook has been reduced from 16 to 3, to avoid storing a large number of empty worksheets.

- Several cells can be merged into one cell. Text in a cell can be indented to provide an informal outline appearance. Data can be angled in a cell or displayed vertically.

Managing Files

Exchanging Files Created in Different Versions of Excel

You can display a file created in an earlier version of Excel simply by opening the file in your current version of Excel. For example, if you have a file that was created in Excel 5.0 and you are currently using Excel 97, open the Excel 5.0 file in Excel 97 to display it.

To convert a file from an earlier version of Excel to a newer version, you must save the file. The following list shows how to save older files into your newer version of Excel:

- **Excel 95.** When you save the file, it is immediately converted into an Excel 95 format.
- **Excel 97.** When you attempt to save a file that was created in an earlier version of Excel, the dialog box displayed in Figure 3.1 appears. You have the choice of saving the file as an Excel 97 file or keeping it as an Excel 5.0 or 95 file.

When you create a file in Excel 95, you do not have to save the file in an Excel 5.0 format in order to open the file in Excel 5.0. Any features unique to Excel 95, such as long filenames, will not be displayed in Excel 5.0. This includes any cell formats that are available only in Excel 95. Figure 3.2 shows the Open dialog box in Excel 5.0. The budget file for 1998 was originally created in Excel 95 and saved as **98 Budget.xls**. Because Windows 3.1 does not allow spaces in filenames and limits the name length to eight characters, **1** the name for this file is converted to **98budg~1.xls**.

When you create a file in Excel 97, you must save the file in an **2** Excel 5.0/95 Workbook or **3** Excel 97 and Excel 5.0/95 Workbook format. This will allow you to open the file in these versions of Excel. Figure 3.3 shows an example of the Save As dialog box in Excel 97 and the choices you have for changing the file type.

> **TIP** Type **converting files** in the Office Assistant (Excel 97) search box for a list of several help screens, including one entitled *Formatting and features not transferred in file conversions.*

60

FIG. 3.1 ▶
Excel 97 update
dialog box

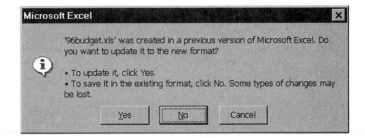

FIG. 3.2 ▶
Excel 5.0 Open
dialog box

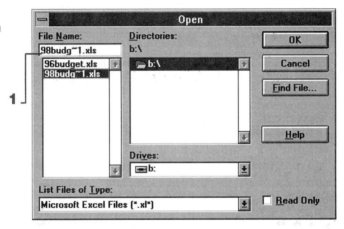

FIG. 3.3 ▶
Excel 97 Save As
dialog box

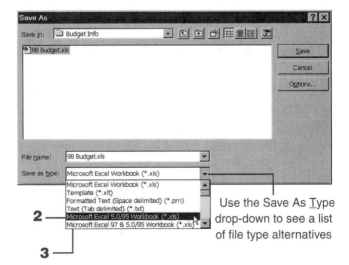

Use the Save As Type
drop-down to see a list
of file type alternatives

Creating New Files Using the Built-in Templates

New in Excel 95 and Excel 97 are a series of predesigned spreadsheet files, which you can use as a starting point for new files. Excel 95 contained 10 templates, whereas Excel 97 contains only three templates. Initially, it may seem odd that there are fewer templates in Excel 97. The three templates in Excel 97 are the most popular templates from Excel 95, and were enhanced and updated for Excel 97. Additionally, new templates and many of the templates from Excel 95 can be downloaded from Microsoft's Excel Free Stuff Web page on the Internet. To download these free templates, choose <u>H</u>elp, Microsoft on the <u>W</u>eb, <u>F</u>ree Stuff.

If you use the New button on the Standard toolbar, the Workbook template is automatically used to create the file. You must use the <u>F</u>ile, <u>N</u>ew command to see a list of the built-in templates.

When you choose the <u>F</u>ile, <u>N</u>ew command in Excel 95 or Excel 97, a dialog box with several tabs appears. The default Workbook template is on the **1** General tab, which contains the default Workbook template. The Spreadsheet Solutions tab, shown in Figure 3.4, contains the predesigned templates. The Spreadsheet Solutions tab in Excel 95 is similar to the one shown in Figure 3.4.

If you have upgraded from Excel 95, the **2** Office 95 templates will be listed on their own tab. This tab appears only if Excel 95 was on your machine when Excel 97 was installed. A **3** preview of the selected template appears on the right side of the dialog box.

When you create a new file based on a template, a copy of the template opens. The templates have sophisticated designs and built-in formulas. Figure 3.5 shows a sample of the Invoice template.

NOTE Some templates contain macros. You may see a warning message that indicates the template contains macros and the computer viruses are usually hidden in macros. This is a very good warning when you open files, especially if those files came from other users or off the Internet.

Choose the Enable Macros button to proceed with displaying a copy of the template.

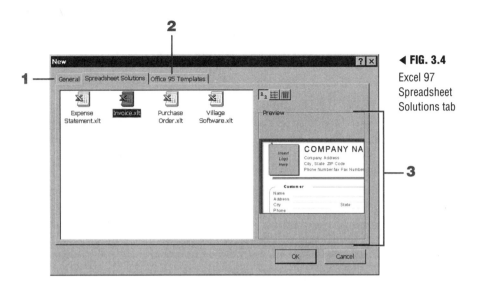

◀ **FIG. 3.4**

Excel 97
Spreadsheet
Solutions tab

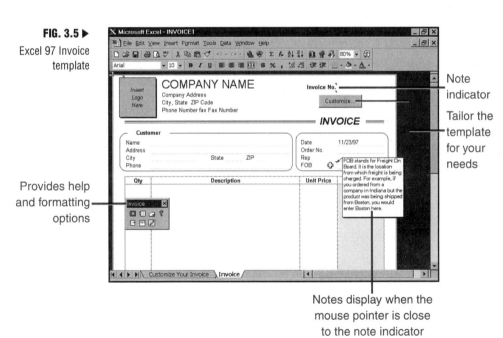

FIG. 3.5 ▶

Excel 97 Invoice
template

Provides help
and formatting
options

Note
indicator

Tailor the
template
for your
needs

Notes display when the
mouse pointer is close
to the note indicator

Saving Files in HTML Format (Excel 97 Only)

New in Excel 97 is the capability to save data and charts from Excel worksheets into a format that can be used for Web pages on the Internet or your company's internal intranet. This format is known as *Hypertext Markup Language* or *HTML*. A wizard will assist you in converting your Excel data into an HTML file.

To access this wizard, choose <u>F</u>ile, Save as <u>H</u>TML. The Internet Assistant Wizard displays the first step in the conversion process, as shown in Figure 3.6. In this step, choose which cells or charts in the Excel worksheet you want to convert. In step 2, shown in Figure 3.7, you can have the data converted into a new file or inserted into an existing HTML file. Figure 3.8 shows step 3 in the Internet Assistant Wizard. In this step, you type information, such as Title, Header, dividing lines, and an email address, that you want to appear in the converted file. Step 4, shown in Figure 3.9, is where you select the location in which you want the converted file to be stored.

FIG. 3.6 ▶
Step 1

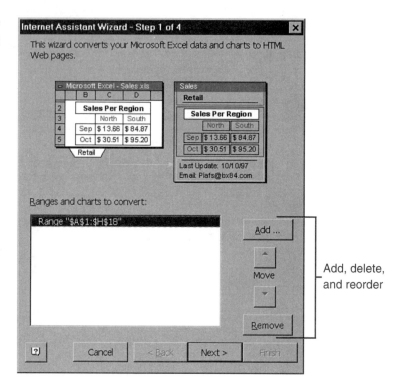

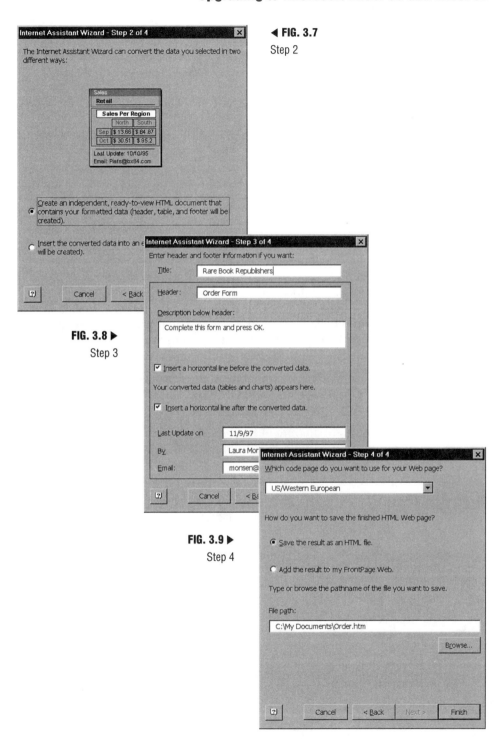

◀ **FIG. 3.7**
Step 2

FIG. 3.8 ▶
Step 3

FIG. 3.9 ▶
Step 4

Editing and Formatting

Merging Cells (Excel 97 Only)

A new feature added to Excel 97 is the capability to merge several cells into one cell. Though merging cells may appear similar to a feature in Excel for centering data across several columns, merging is, in fact, quite different. Figure 3.10 illustrates both **1** merged cells and **2** centered data.

Merging physically combines several cells into one cell in the worksheet. Centering data across several columns simply changes the display of the data; the cells remain unchanged.

When cells are merged, the upper-leftmost cell reference becomes the reference for the merged cells. In the first example of merged cells in Figure 3.10, the cell reference for the merged cells is B2 (C2, D2, and E2 no longer exist).

If the cells you select to merge contain data, only the data in the upper-left cell of the selected group of cells is retained when the cells are merged. Excel will warn you that all other data will be lost if you proceed to merge the cells. In Figure 3.10, **3** the cells B7 through D8 have been selected. The **4** warning message appears when you attempt to merge the cells. If the cells are merged in this example, only **1997** is retained, while **Budget** is lost.

The Center Across Columns button, available on the Formatting toolbar in Excel 5.0 and Excel 95, has become **5** Merge and Center in Excel 97. When you use this button, the selected cells are merged, and the data is centered in the merged cells.

Use the Left, Center, or Right alignment buttons on the Formatting toolbar to change the horizontal alignment of data in the merged cells.

> **NOTE** The **6** Merge Cells option is also available on the Alignment tab in the Format Cells dialog box (see Figure 3.11).
>
> Use the **7** Horizontal alignment options in the Format Cells dialog box to center data across several columns.

To split cells that have been merged, clear the Merge Cells check box on the Alignment tab of the Format Cells dialog box (see Figure 3.11).

FIG. 3.10 ▶
Merged cells

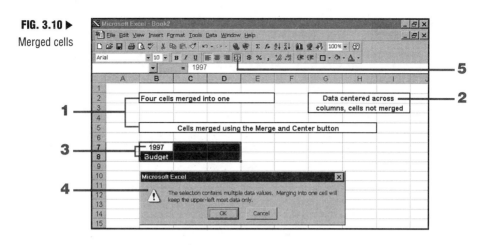

◀ FIG. 3.11
Format Cells
dialog box

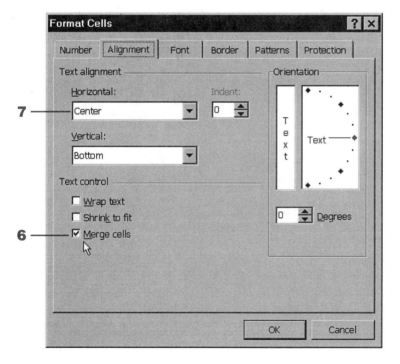

Editing and Formatting

Indenting and Rotating Data (Excel 97 Only)

To enhance the appearance of the data in your worksheets, Excel 97 includes two new formatting options: indenting and rotating.

Data can be indented inside a cell, up to 15 levels. You can rotate data in a cell from 90 degrees to –90 degrees, at 1-degree increments, or display the data vertically.

To indent or rotate data, choose Format, Cells. From the Alignment tab (see Figure 3.12), select the desired **1** levels of indention or **2** degrees of rotation. Instead of rotating the data, you can change its orientation data to **3** vertical.

You can also indent data with the **4** Decrease Indent and **5** Increase Indent buttons on the Formatting toolbar, shown in Figure 3.13.

Figure 3.13 shows an example of using **6** rotating and **7** indenting data to enhance a worksheet.

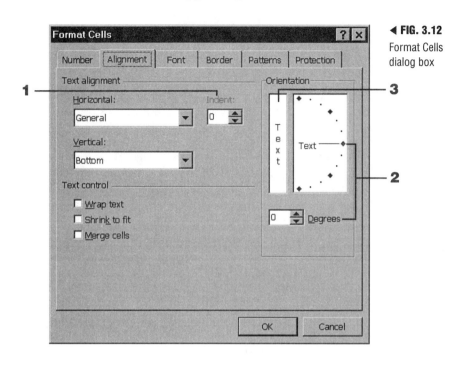

◄ **FIG. 3.12**
Format Cells
dialog box

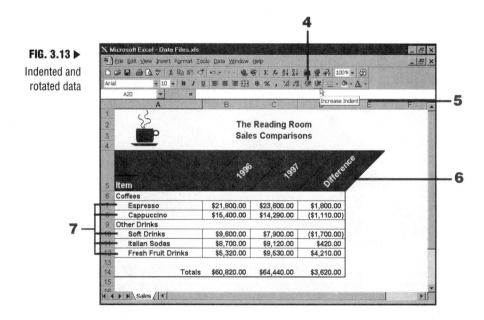

FIG. 3.13 ►
Indented and
rotated data

Editing and Formatting

AutoComplete

You will spend less time with data entry in Excel by using the AutoComplete feature. If you have repetitive text entries in a particular column, AutoComplete can help you enter the text more quickly, especially when the entries differ after the second or third letter. AutoComplete is available in Excel 95 and Excel 97. AutoComplete compares the characters you type in a cell with entries in the same column, above and below the active cell. If there is another text entry that matches the characters you have typed, AutoComplete fills in the remaining characters. If AutoComplete fills in the entry you want, press Enter; otherwise, continue to type your entry.

The example in Figure 3.14 shows a list of book orders and a list of music orders. Several of the cities begin with the letters *Ca*: **Calgary**, **Calcutta**, **Canberra**, **Cairo**, and **Cannes**. If you type **Can** in cell A10, AutoComplete fills in the remaining letters of the city **Canberra**. Although Cannes also begins with *Can* in column A, Excel looks only for entries that are in a continuous list and stops at the point where a blank cell is encountered. Because there is at least one blank line between the list of city names in Figure 3.14, none of the city names in the second list will be proposed by AutoComplete when entering names in the first list.

AutoComplete duplicates the capitalization used in the first occurrence of the word. In this example, if you type **ca**, where the letter *c* is not capitalized, Canberra will be capitalized when you press Enter.

NOTE AutoComplete does not work with numbers.

FIG. 3.14 ▶

Excel 95 and 97
AutoComplete

AutoComplete
proposes the
remaining text

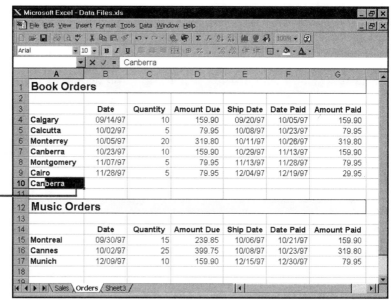

Editing and Formatting

Validating Data Entry (Excel 97 Only)

The Data Validation command is a new, powerful feature in Excel 97. Through this command, you have three options for controlling data entry:

- You can control the data that can be entered in a cell by displaying a list of choices or by placing restrictions (limits) on the entries.
- You can create input messages that instruct users on the appropriate data to be entered in a cell.
- You can display an error message if incorrect data is entered in a cell or have Excel draw circles around invalid entries in the worksheet.

You can use these three options separately or in conjunction with one another.

To validate the data that is entered in a cell, choose Data, Validation. The Settings tab, shown in Figure 3.15, is where you select the type of data you want to allow in the cell. The **1** validation criteria options displayed on the Settings tab change based on your selection.

The **2** Input Message tab of the Data Validation dialog box is used to create a message that instructs users on the type of data expected in the cell. The **3** Error Alert tab of the Data Validation dialog box is used to create a message that displays when an invalid entry is made. Choose the Circle Invalid Data button on the Auditing toolbar to draw circles around cells in the worksheet.

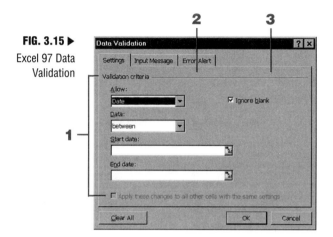

FIG. 3.15 ▶

Excel 97 Data
Validation

Applying Conditional Formats (Excel 97 Only)

A powerful new number-formatting feature has been added to Excel 97 that makes it easy to format a cell based on the data in the cell. Conditional formatting is especially useful for highlighting the results of formulas. You can specify up to three conditional formats for a cell.

Figure 3.16 shows the appearance of a worksheet before and after conditional formatting. In this example:

- If the % Change is negative, the cell displays light gray shading. The % Change for **1** Colorado has gray shading.
- If the % Change is between 5% and 15%, the cell displays in bold font. The % Change for **2** Virginia is in bold.
- If the % Change is 15% or higher, the cell displays in bold and italic. The % Change for **3** Wyoming is displayed in bold and italic.

There is no specific condition if the % Change is between 0% and 5% (therefore, the cells for California and Texas); the formatting that already exists in the cell remains.

The Conditional Formatting dialog box, shown in Figure 3.17, lists the formats applied to the % Change cells in Figure 3.16. Choose Format, Conditional Formatting to access this dialog box.

NOTE If conditional formatting is added to a cell that has a formula, when the formula is copied, the conditional formatting is copied, too.

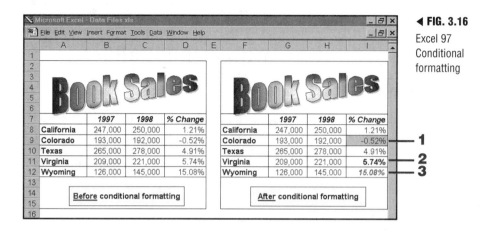

◀ **FIG. 3.16**

Excel 97
Conditional
formatting

FIG. 3.17 ▶

Conditional
Formatting dialog
box

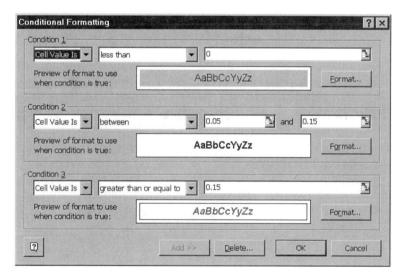

Displaying and Reviewing Embedded Comments

Attaching notes to cells is a feature that has been available since Excel 5.0. In both Excel 95 and Excel 97, this feature was enhanced; in Excel 97, it was renamed *Comments*. Attaching comments to cells is especially useful in forms or templates inside of which other people will be inputting data. Comments are a means of preventing errors and providing explanations in worksheets.

Figure 3.18 shows a worksheet with built-in comments. Comments can be attached to any cell. Excel places **1** an indicator in the upper-right corner of each cell that contains a comment. The indicator is a red triangle. New in Excel 95, when you position the mouse pointer in the cell, the comment automatically appears on the screen. In Excel 97, **2** the author of the comment is included with the comment, and **3** a new toolbar, the Reviewing toolbar, has been designed especially for creating and reading comments.

To create or edit a comment in Excel 95, choose Insert, Note. In Excel 97, choose Insert, Comment.

> **TIP** The bold title in the comment is taken from the User Name box on the General tab of the Options dialog box. You can edit the text directly in the comment in the worksheet, making each title unique to that particular comment.

To print worksheet comments, choose File, Page Setup, and select the Sheet tab in the Page Setup dialog box. Comments are printed on a separate page. In Excel 97 you can print the comments in the worksheet. You must first display the comments on the worksheet by choosing the Comment and Indicator setting on the View tab of the Options dialog box.

> **NOTE** The Page Setup dialog box must be accessed from the File menu, not through the Print Preview screen, to choose one of the Comment print options.

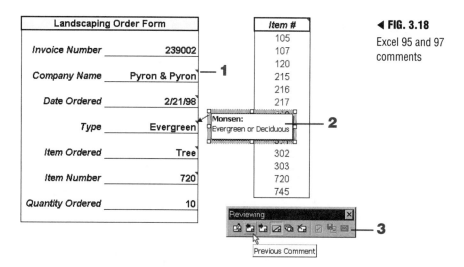

◀ **FIG. 3.18**

Excel 95 and 97 comments

Formulas and Functions

Creating and Editing Formulas (Excel 97 Only)

Several new enhancements have been added to Excel 97 that make it easier to create and edit formulas, especially if you use worksheet functions. In Excel 5.0 and Excel 95, when you want to use a function, you either type in the function or select the Function Wizard button on the Standard toolbar. In Excel 97, **1** Paste Function replaces the Function Wizard. The Paste Function command expands on the features that were part of the Function Wizard, making it easier to use the built-in worksheet functions.

Figure 3.19 shows the **2** Paste Function dialog box. The **3** Office Assistant appears, asking if you need help using the dialog box. If you don't know which function to use, select Yes in the Office Assistant pop-up and type a description of what you want to do. The Office Assistant will suggest which worksheet functions to use.

Once you select the function to use, choose OK. A dialog box for the function you selected appears (see Figure 3.20). This dialog box is referred to as the Formula Palette. The Paste Function dialog box is anchored below the **4** Formula Bar. This dialog box displays **5** a description of the function and each argument.

Often, Excel selects the range of cells to use in the function. In this example, Excel has **6** selected cells B4:B15. This would create an inaccurate average, because the Year Total in cell B15 is included in the range. A new feature in this dialog box enables you to **7** collapse the dialog box to more easily select cells in your worksheet. Once you have selected the cells, you can then expand the dialog box by using the same button.

> **TIP** You cannot select range names from the Name box on the Formula Bar while the Formula Palette is displayed. To include range names in a formula, press F3.

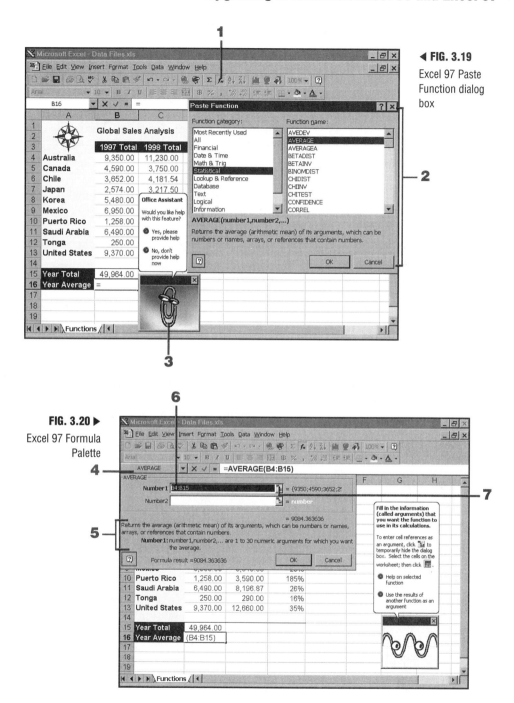

◀ FIG. 3.19
Excel 97 Paste Function dialog box

FIG. 3.20 ▶
Excel 97 Formula Palette

Formulas and Functions

New Functions (Excel 97 Only)

Several new functions have been added in Excel 97. All functions available to older versions of Excel are available to Excel 97. Figure 3.21 compares the AVERAGE function to the AVERAGEA function. The **1** formula for the AVERAGEA function appears in the Formula Bar. The following table lists new functions found in Excel 97:

- **AVERAGEA.** Similar to AVERAGE. Returns the average of the values in a range of cells. In addition to numbers, cells that contain text and logical values such as TRUE and FALSE are included in the calculation, which AVERAGE does not do.

- **GETPIVOTDATA.** Retrieves data from a PivotTable.

- **HYPERLINK.** Creates a shortcut or jump that opens a document stored on a network server, an intranet, or the Internet.

- **MAXA.** Similar to MAX. Returns the largest value in a range of cells. In addition to numbers, cells that contain text and logical values such as TRUE and FALSE are included in the calculation, which MAX does not do.

- **MINA.** Similar to MIN. Returns the minimum value in a range of cells. In addition to numbers, cells that contain text and logical values such as TRUE and FALSE are included in the calculation, which MIN does not do.

- **STDEVA.** Similar to STDEV. Estimates standard deviation based on a sample of a population. In addition to numbers, cells that contain text and logical values such as TRUE and FALSE are included in the calculation, which STDEV does not do.

- **STDEVPA.** Similar to STDEVP. Calculates standard deviation based on an entire population. In addition to numbers, cells that contain text and logical values such as TRUE and FALSE are included in the calculation, which STDEVP does not do.

- **VARA.** Similar to VAR. Estimates the variance of a sample of a population. In addition to numbers, cells that contain text and logical values such as TRUE and FALSE are included in the calculation, which VAR does not do.

- **VARPA.** Similar to VARP. Calculates the variance based on the entire population. In addition to numbers, cells that contain text and logical values such as TRUE and FALSE are included in the calculation, which VARP does not do.

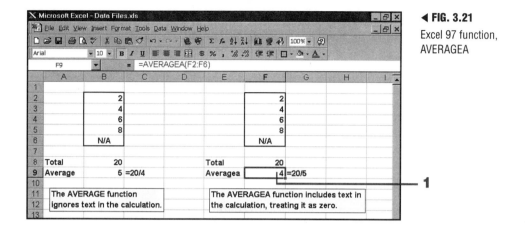

◀ FIG. 3.21

Excel 97 function, AVERAGEA

Analyzing Worksheets

Filtering Lists

The AutoFilter feature was introduced in Excel 5.0 (Office 4.3), making it easier to display a *subset* of a list of information in Excel. AutoFilter displays multiple rows (records) matching criteria you specify. You can filter based on an item in the list or create a custom filter in which you can include AND and OR conditions.

In Excel 95, a new option—Top 10—was added to AutoFilter. This feature displays the ten most common values in the selected column. The Top 10 filter is identical in Excel 95 and Excel 97.

Figure 3.22 shows an Excel 97 list of employee information with the **1** AutoFilter active. A filter showing the employees who earn the **Top 15 Percent** of all salaries has been applied to the list. The **2** Top 10 AutoFilter dialog box shows the criteria selected for this filter. Although the name implies you can display the top ten, you actually have much more flexibility than that:

- **3 Portion of the list.** Choose to display the Top or Bottom portion of the list.
- **4 Amount.** Choose any number between 1 and 500.
- **5 Type of information.** Choose to display the amount of items or the amount as a percentage of the whole list.

Figure 3.23 shows the same list of employees, this time with the **Top 15 Items** as the criteria for the filter.

> **NOTE**   The Top 10 AutoFilter can be used only on columns that contain numbers or dates. It cannot be applied to columns that contain text.

FIG. 3.22 ▶

Excel 97—Top 10 AutoFilter displaying a percent

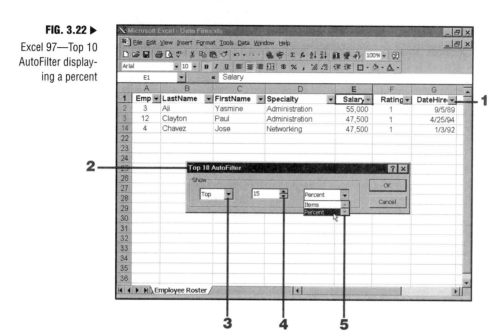

◀ FIG. 3.23

Excel 97—Top 10 AutoFilter displaying a number of items

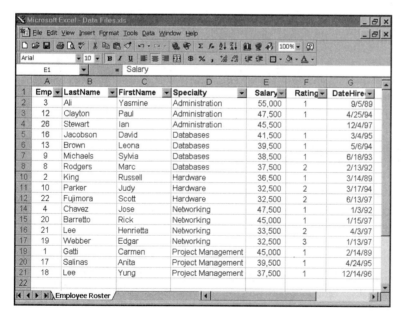

Analyzing Worksheets

Pivot Table Improvements

Pivot tables, a new feature in Excel 5.0, replaces the crosstab tables feature in earlier versions of Excel. The PivotTable Wizard was included in Excel 5.0 to assist users in selecting data for the pivot table and continues to be a valuable tool in Excel 95 and Excel 97.

Many pivot table enhancements have been added in Excel 97. Options that affect the entire pivot table are controlled in a separate PivotTable Options dialog box, as shown in Figure 3.24. You can access this dialog box from the final step (step 4 of 4) in the PivotTable Wizard or from the **1** PivotTable button on the PivotTable toolbar (see Figure 3.25). Some of the enhancements made to Excel pivot tables include the following:

- **Selecting part of a pivot table.** You can select parts of the pivot table structure to format or use in formulas using the **2** Select command.
- **Calculated fields and items.** Creating calculated fields and items is located under the **3** Formulas command on the PivotTable toolbar.
- **Automatic sorting.** Items in a pivot table can be sorted automatically, even when the pivot table layout is changed. **4** Choose PivotTable, Field on the PivotTable toolbar and click the Advanced button to locate the sorting options.
- **Page field retrieval options.** When the pivot table is extracting data from a large external database, you can extract each item in a page field as you display that item. **4** Choose PivotTable, Field on the PivotTable toolbar and click the Advanced button to locate the retrieval options.
- **Formatting.** When you apply formatting and AutoFormats to selected parts of a pivot table, the formatting remains even when you refresh the data or change the pivot table layout by using Preserve Formatting under the **5** Options command on the PivotTable toolbar.
- **Errors values or empty cells.** When a pivot table generates an error value or an empty cell, you can program Excel to display something else in the pivot table. The Error value and empty cell options are located under the **5** Options command on the PivotTable toolbar.
- **Running background queries.** You can run a query on an external database in the background so that you can continue working in Microsoft Excel while the data is being retrieved for a pivot table. The Background Queries option is located under the **5** Options command.
- **Using pivot table data in formulas.** The new GETPIVOTDATA worksheet function lets you create formulas that perform calculations using data in pivot tables.

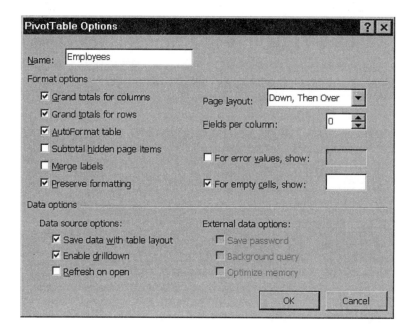

◀ FIG. 3.24

Excel 97
PivotTable
options

FIG. 3.25 ▶

Excel 97
PivotTable
toolbar

Using the Built-in Templates

A *template* is a special type of workbook file that is used as a master, or blueprint, for creating other Excel workbooks. Both Excel 95 and Excel 97 include built-in worksheet templates that provide common spreadsheet forms such as invoices, purchase orders, and expense statements.

Excel 95 contains 10 predesigned templates: Business Planner, Car Lease Advisor, Change Request, Expense Statement, Invoice, Loan Manager, Personal Budgeter, Purchase Order, Sales Quote, and Time Card.

In Excel 97, three of these templates have been updated and are included with the standard installation of the software: Expense Statement, Invoice, and Purchase Order. You can copy the other seven templates from the Office 97 CD or download them from Microsoft's Web site.

To access the built-in templates, choose File, New. The New dialog box displays a series of tabs that identify the templates available in Excel (see Figure 3.26). The **1** General tab lists the Workbook template, used as the default template for new workbooks. The **2** Spreadsheet Solutions tab lists the built-in templates. If you have upgraded from Office 95 to Office 97, the **3** Office 95 Templates tab also may be listed in the New dialog box.

In Figure 3.27, a new workbook has been created based on the built-in Invoice template. Templates can be **4** customized to fit your specific requirements. Each built-in template has an option to **5** include your company name and logo. You also can change the font and add your own comments. Most templates include **6** a toolbar to help you with the template. Some of the built-in templates include **7** a feature that enables you to add data to a database each time you complete the template form. **8** Helpful notes and tips embedded in the templates assist you in working with and customizing the templates.

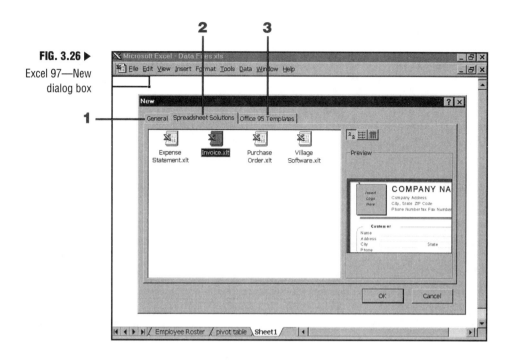

FIG. 3.26 ▶

Excel 97—New
dialog box

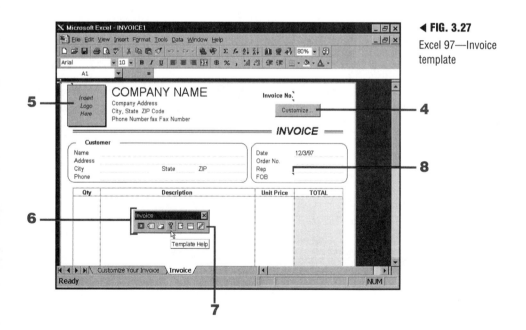

◀ FIG. 3.27

Excel 97—Invoice
template

Template Wizard with Data Tracking

The Template Wizard with Data Tracking is a new add-in feature available in Excel 95 and 97. *Add-ins* are supplemental programs that add custom commands and features to Excel. The Template Wizard is used to link cells in a worksheet to fields in a database. This is particularly useful with templates that are input forms. When the form is filled in, a corresponding record is created in a database. The information in the database then can be manipulated by using the features of the database.

Some of the built-in templates include a feature that enables you to add data to a database each time you complete the template form. The data is added as a new record in a database that is associated with the template. You also can add your own custom templates that will store data into a database by using the Template Wizard with Data Tracking. The database can be a list in Excel or a database in Access, FoxPro, dBASE, or Paradox.

For example, suppose that you want to track the hours that employees worked each week on client projects. You would design a work log form on a worksheet and use the Template Wizard to create the template and links to a database. When the employee completes the work-log form, the copy of the form can be saved or printed. The completed work-log data is copied to the corresponding data fields as a new record in the database.

Additionally, you can use this feature with multiple sites that are connected by a network, where the form is linked to a central database. Store the template on a shared network drive to make it available to all users. You will need to create a shortcut to the template and make sure the shortcut is copied to the Templates folder on each user's desktop.

The Template Wizard contains five steps, with explanations to guide you through the wizard (see Figure 3.28). Follow the steps in the wizard to create the data-tracking links.

FIG. 3.28 ►

Excel 97
Template Wizard

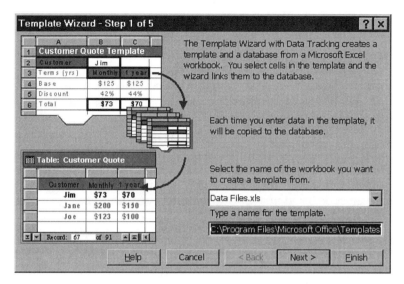

Charts and Maps

Creating Maps

New in Microsoft Excel 95 (and included in Office 97) is a feature you can use to create a map based on your worksheet data. Maps can be created to analyze sales, marketing, or any other data that is broken out geographically. The mapping feature includes demographic data, such as population and household income, that can be used along with your data.

When you create a map, the first step is to set up and select the data you want to display. Arrange the information to be mapped in columns on a worksheet. You must have at least one column that contains the names of geographic areas, countries, or states. If you want to plot additional data, such as sales figures, this data must be listed in a separate column. When you select the cells to plot in the map, include the column headings.

Figure 3.29 shows an example of a map of the United States. To use the mapping feature, select the range of cells on your worksheet and click the **1** Map button on the Standard toolbar. Then drag a rectangular shape in your worksheet where you want the map to appear.

You can change the colors and formats displayed in the map, add custom labels, or change the map's legends. For more information about working with maps, **2** click the callouts on the "Displaying data in a map" help screen (see Figure 3.30).

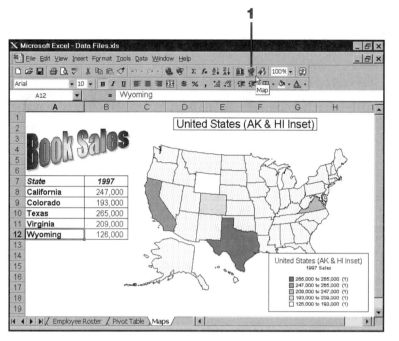

◀ **FIG. 3.29**

Excel 95 and
Excel 97 sample
map

FIG. 3.30 ▶

Online help for
mapping

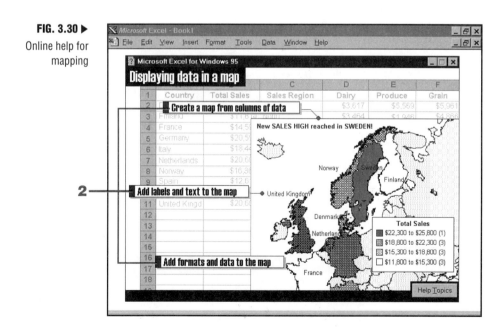

Charts and Maps

Improved Chart Wizard (Excel 97 Only)

The Chart Wizard in Excel 95 is virtually identical to and has the same capabilities as the Chart Wizard in Excel 5.0. In Excel 97, the Chart Wizard has improved greatly. You can create both embedded charts and chart sheets with the wizard. There are many new and enhanced options, and the Office Assistant is programmed to provide assistance as you build your chart.

There are 14 standard chart types available in Excel 97. The **1** Cylinder, Cone, and Pyramid chart types are variations of the column and bar charts, as shown in Figure 3.31. Figure 3.31 shows step 1 of 4 of the new Chart Wizard, with the Pyramid chart type selected. Another chart type new to Excel 97 is the Bubble, a type of scatter chart. Pie of Pie and Bar of Pie are variations of the Pie chart used to further break out specific components of a wedge of the original pie.

In addition to the standard chart types, you can use 20 custom chart types. You will find special types like Combination charts and Logarithmic charts under the custom types, as well as some of the standard chart types that have been modified with colorful backgrounds or shading.

Other improvements to charts in Excel 97 include the following:

- Easier editing of embedded charts.
- Data tables now available in charts.
- Number of data points plotted per series increased from 4,000 to 32,000.
- New formatting options, such as using pictures or texture for fills and scaling marker size. Figure 3.32 shows an example of a picture fill used in a bar chart.
- **2** Chart tips available when you rest the mouse pointer over a chart object.
- Improved display of text in charts, including **3** text rotation.

> **TIP** Excel provides a number of good chart examples through the built-in help screens: Type **chart examples** in the Office Assistant search box and choose **Examples of chart types**.

FIG. 3.31 ▶
Excel 97 Chart
Wizard

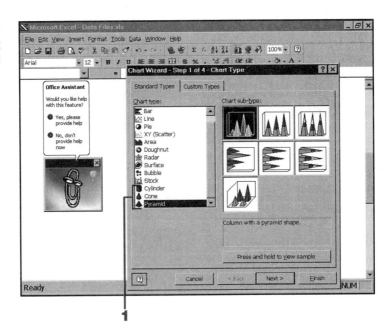

◀ FIG. 3.32
Excel 97 bar chart

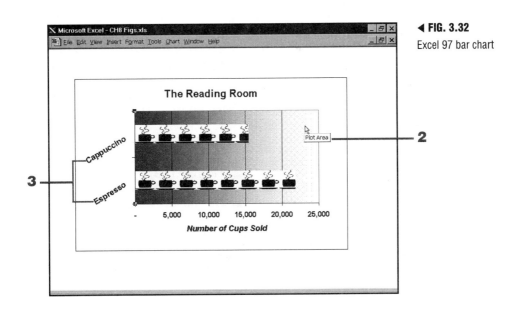

Workgroup Features
Sharing Workbooks

One of the most productive features in Excel is the capability to share and revise workbooks with groups of people. Frequently, projects involve several people entering or verifying data in the same documents.

In Excel 5.0 (Office 4.3), your only options for sharing a workbook are saving the workbook to a network drive or electronically mailing/routing the workbook to other users. Either way, you cannot easily track what changes were made and by whom.

In Excel 95, you have the ability to share your workbooks with other users and track the changes made to the workbook. The File, Shared Lists command is used to share the workbook and determine who has the file open. With this command, you can enter data or sort data, add rows or columns, but you cannot change cell formatting or modify formulas. If changes made to the file conflict, you can see a list of conflicts and determine which changes to accept or reject. You continue to have the option of routing the workbook electronically to other users for their review.

In Excel 97, you have the ability to truly share a workbook. One person can edit one worksheet in a workbook, and someone else can edit another worksheet simultaneously. When one user saves the workbook, the other users who are sharing it will see the changes made by that user. Different people can access adjacent data in the same worksheet, such as the formulas on a worksheet and the column headings. The shared workbook feature replaces the shared list feature in Microsoft Excel 95. Excel 97 provides several options you can use when you need to coordinate workbook files with groups of people: creating a Binder file, sharing workbooks, tracking changes, and highlighting text.

> **TIP** Only Excel 97 supports the shared workbook feature. If some users in your group are still working with previous versions of Excel, they will not be able to open the shared workbook.

To share a workbook with other users in Excel 97, choose Tools, Share Workbook, and the Share Workbook dialog box appears (see Figure 3.33). The Advanced tab contains sharing options that control how changes to the shared workbook will be tracked. When a workbook is shared, the word [Shared] appears in the title bar for the workbook.

The Highlight Changes dialog box, shown in Figure 3.34, works with settings on the Advanced tab of the Share Workbook dialog box to control how changes to the shared workbook are tracked.

Each time you view the shared workbook, you need to specify how you want to review the changes in the Highlight Changes dialog box. The settings are established only for the working session; the next time you view the file, you have to specify your choices again. Some Excel commands are not available when a workbook is shared:

- **Inserting and Deleting.** Blocks of cells cannot be inserted or deleted, though you can insert or delete entire rows and columns. You can insert worksheets but cannot delete worksheets.

- **Formatting.** You cannot apply conditional formats or merged cells after a workbook has been shared.

- **List Manipulation Commands.** When you filter data in a shared workbook and make print settings you want, your settings are then saved independently of settings made by other users. Whenever you open the shared workbook, your personal settings appear. The Group and Outline, Subtotals, Tables, and PivotTable Report commands cannot be used when a workbook is shared.

- **Linked or Embedded Objects.** Charts, pictures, objects, or hyperlinks can't be modified in a shared workbook.

- **Macros.** You can only run macros that were created before you shared the workbook. New macros cannot be created.

- **Password Protection.** While a workbook is shared, you cannot create, modify, or remove passwords that protect the worksheets or the entire workbook. Any protection that is assigned to a worksheet or workbook prior to sharing the file remains in effect while the workbook is shared.

- **Scenarios.** This command can't be used while the workbook is shared.

- **Data Validation.** You can't modify or create data-validation restrictions while the workbook is shared. Any restrictions that are set up prior to sharing the workbook remain in effect.

- **Drawing.** The drawing tools can't be used after a workbook has been shared.

Most of the limitations can be implemented before sharing the workbook, and then are available after sharing the workbook.

When users make changes to your workbook, their edits are color coded. When you rest the pointer over a cell that has been modified, information is displayed about who made the change, when the change was made, and what type of change it was.

> **TIP** Excel identifies who made what changes, when in the shared workbook, based on the name of the user. To ensure accurate tracking, each user should establish his or her user name before working on the shared book. Instruct each user to choose Tools, Options and click the General tab, and then type his or her user name in the User Name box.

You can step through highlighted changes in a shared workbook and accept or reject each change. Information about how conflicts are resolved is now available on the History worksheet (the Conflicts worksheet in Excel 95). The History worksheet maintains information about any changes that are replaced by other changes. You can track the history of changes to a shared workbook for a specified amount of time. When you want to view what changes have been made to the workbook, you can display a separate filtered History worksheet.

If you reject a change, you can get it back by finding it in the History worksheet for the workbook.

NOTE When you remove a workbook from shared use, the history of changes is erased. When you share the workbook again, a new list of changes is created.

Users can attach their comments directly to cells. In Excel 5.0 and Excel 95, these are called Notes. In Excel 97, they are called Comments. Figure 3.35 shows a **1** shared workbook with several **2** embedded comments. One of the features added to Comments in Excel 97 is the **3** Reviewing toolbar. You can use this toolbar to make sure you've read all the comments by stepping through the comments in a workbook in sequence.

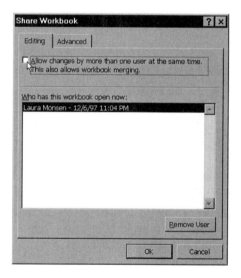

FIG. 3.33 ▶

Excel 97—Share Workbook dialog box

FIG. 3.34 ▶
Excel 97—
Highlight Changes
dialog box

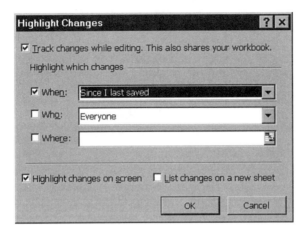

◀ FIG. 3.35
A shared work-
book with embed-
ded comments

Commentator
indicator

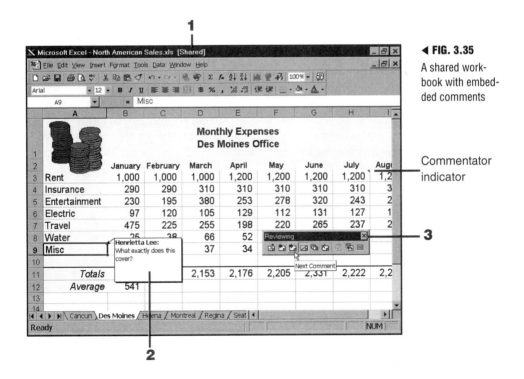

Merging Workbooks (Excel 97 Only)

Instead of sharing a workbook with other users, you can provide separate copies of a workbook to users and then merge the copies, along with any comments or changes, into one workbook file. This feature is not available to Excel 5.0 and Excel 95 users.

Before you distribute copies of the workbook for review and editing, there are several things to consider:

- The workbook from which the copies are to be made must be a shared workbook.
- All copies must come from the same workbook but must have unique filenames.
- Before the copies are made, the change history in the original workbook must be turned on (choose the Advanced tab in the Share Workbooks dialog box). Then the merge must be completed within the time period you specified to maintain the history. If you aren't sure how long the review process will take, make sure you enter a large number of days, such as 500.
- The workbooks either must not have passwords or must both have the same password.

When workbooks are merged, comments on a cell from different users are identified by individual user names and are merged into a single comment box. Choose Tools, Merge Workbooks to merge your workbooks (see Figure 3.36).

> **NOTE**   You can use the Merge Workbooks command with the My Briefcase feature to edit a copy of a workbook on your laptop, and then merge your changes back into the copy of the workbook on your network or office desktop.

FIG. 3.36 ▶

Excel 97—Select
Files to Merge
Into Current
Workbook dialog
box

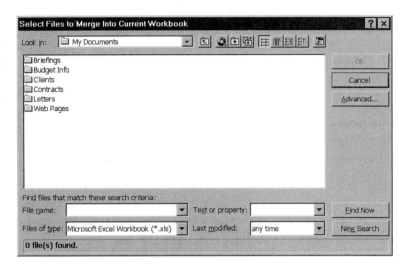

Importing and Exporting Data
Converting Excel Data into Access

You can import files from many different programs by simply using the File, Open command. Excel files can be exported to other programs by saving them in other file formats through the File, Save As command. This feature is available in all versions of Excel.

Both Excel 95 and Excel 97 come with the capability to create Access forms and reports based on your Excel worksheets, while you are in Excel. The AccessLinks Add-In contains wizards that prompt you through the process of creating Access forms and reports. Additionally, this add-in includes the Convert to Access command, which enables you to move data from Excel worksheets to an Access database.

In Excel 95, the AccessLinks Add-In is automatically installed and is comprised of three commands on the Data menu: Access Form, Access Report, and Convert to Access.

In Excel 97, you will have to install the AccessLinks Add-In. Choose Tools, Add-Ins and select AccessLinks from the Add-In dialog box. The MS Access Form, MS Access Report, and Convert to MS Access commands will then be added to the Data menu.

The Access Form and Access Report commands work similarly. When you select one of these commands, it launches a wizard. The wizard will guide you through building a data entry form or a report based on your Excel list. To create the form or report, a table will be created in Access based on the data in your Excel list. When you select either the Access Form or Access Report command, a dialog box appears asking whether you want to create the form or report in a new Access database or an existing Access database. Figure 3.37 shows the Create Microsoft Access Form dialog box. The Create Microsoft Access Report dialog box is identical, except for the title of the dialog box.

> **NOTE** Your data must be organized as a list (or database) in Excel before you attempt to use the Access Form or Access Report commands. An Excel list begins with a row of headings and cannot contain any empty rows or columns. The headings will be used by Access as field names in the new table.

Once you have made your selections in the dialog box, the **1** Access program is opened, and a table based on your Excel list is created. Then the Form or Report Wizard starts, using the **2** newly created table. Figure 3.38 shows the first step in the Access Form Wizard. Figure 3.39 shows the first step in the Access Report Wizard.

After the form or report is created, the wizard adds a button to your Excel worksheet. You can modify the form or report by using this button.

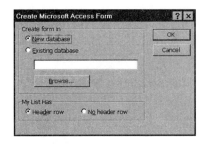

◀ FIG. 3.37

Excel 97—Access
Form Wizard

FIG. 3.38 ▶

Excel 97—Select
the fields to
include in the
form

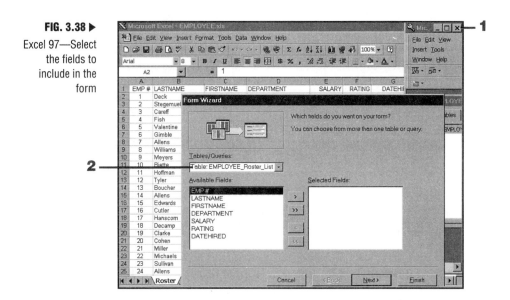

◀ FIG. 3.39

Excel 97—Select
the fields to
include in the
report

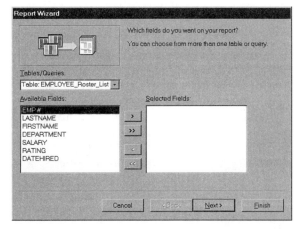

101

Enhanced MS Query (Excel 97 Only)

An extremely powerful feature of Excel is the capability to retrieve data from external sources so that it can be analyzed and manipulated by the tools in Excel. Microsoft Query has been available in Excel since version 5.0. It is a separate program that comes with Microsoft Office and that works with Excel to make it easy to retrieve data from databases and copy the data into an Excel worksheet. You can then use any of the tools Excel provides, such as pivot tables and charting, to work with the list of data. In Excel 97, the integration between Microsoft Query and Excel has been improved.

You can access Microsoft Query directly from Excel to retrieve specific information from external sources, primarily databases. Some examples of the programs you can retrieve data from include Access, FoxPro, dBASE, Paradox, and SQL Server. In Excel 97, you also can retrieve information from the Internet by using HTML filters. The data can be filtered, sorted, formatted, or edited in Microsoft Query *before* it is inserted into your worksheet. The data can be retrieved by using either the Query Wizard, a new interface in Microsoft Query available only in Excel 97, or directly from the Microsoft Query window using Excel 95 or Excel 97. The Query Wizard helps you create quick and simple query designs to retrieve data; use it when you want to retrieve data from only *one table* in a database. If you want to retrieve data from *multiple tables* in a database, the Microsoft Query window enables you to work in more detail to customize and view your data retrieval.

To start Microsoft Query, choose Data, Get External Data, Create New Query. The Choose Data Source dialog box appears, as shown in Figure 3.40.

> **NOTE**   Microsoft Query is an optional feature in Microsoft Excel and may not be installed on your computer. If a warning message appears when you select Create New Query, then Microsoft Query is not installed. You will have to install Microsoft Query from the Microsoft Office disks or CD before you can proceed.

You can create and distribute queries to other Excel 97 users, so they don't have to repeat the steps of setting up the data source to run the query. A worksheet can be saved with a query as a template, without saving a copy of the retrieved data. When you open the report template, the external data is retrieved. You will be prompted for a password if one is required. Queries can be created that prompt you for parameters each time they're run, so that you can create more flexible queries and work with larger databases. Queries now run in the background so that you can continue to work on other things in Excel while data is being retrieved.

FIG. 3.40 ▶
Excel 97—
Choose Data
Source dialog box

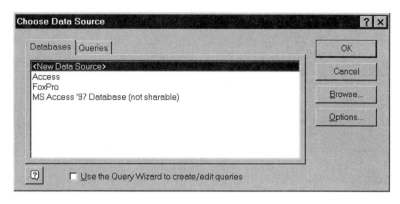

4

Upgrading to Microsoft Access 95 and Access 97

Significant improvements to Access have been made since the release of Access 2.0 in Office 4.3. Most of the changes made to Access came between Access 2.0 and Access 95. Access 97 incorporates the improvements made to Access 95 and adds some new features.

New and enhanced features found in Access 97 include:

- **What's New.** Learn about all the new and exciting features that have been added to Access.

- **Managing Files.** Convert files created in previous versions of Access to your current version of Access. Save your Access files in HTML format so that they can be used as Web pages.

- **Databases.** Get acquainted with the new Database window. Create entire new databases using built-in templates, which include tables, forms, reports, and queries.

- **Tables and Records.** Create tables using the improved wizards or directly in the Design and Datasheet Views. Discover the new Lookup Wizard and Hyperlink field data types.

- **Queries.** Explore the advantages of using the Design View to create and modify your queries.

- **Reports.** Create multitable reports without creating a query first. Learn to use the group and report sections to create subtotals and grand totals in your reports.

- **Forms.** Take advantage of the wizards to build input forms, including subforms.

- **Builders.** Create powerful expressions for queries and reports in the Expression Builder.

- **Importing and Exporting.** Exchange data with Excel and other programs effortlessly.

What's New

Access 95

The most significant changes in Access have taken place in Access 95. The following list describes many of these new or enhanced features:

- **Interface.** Some menus and dialog boxes have been redesigned to make them easier to use and to correspond with the other Office 95 programs. Several commands have been renamed. The Database Window moves more quickly between the database objects. You can alter the icons and amount of information about the objects by using four list types.

- **Wizards.** Many new or improved wizards have been added to Access. The Database Wizard enables you to create an entire, professional database using built-in templates. The Lookup Wizard helps you to create a lookup field in a table. You can split a large table into smaller more efficient tables using the Table Analyzer Wizard, which is especially useful for tables created by importing data from Excel. A PivotTable Wizard has been included to create a PivotTable control on a form.

- **Filtering.** Choose from several new filtering options, including Filtering by Form and Filtering by Selection.

- **Security.** Assign one password to control user access to a database instead of, or in addition to, implementing user-level security. A new User-Level Security Wizard makes it easier to protect your database.

Additional enhancements and changes in Access 95 include the following:

- Use the AutoFormat feature to quickly change the look of reports and forms.

- Using replication, users can work on their own copies of the database and then modifications made in all copies can be synchronized.

- When you save a table, query, or form that has been sorted, Access saves the sort order. New forms or reports based on a sorted table or query inherit the sort order.

- You can drag tables and queries from the Database window to other applications, such as Microsoft Excel or Word.

- The Archive Query is no longer available. You can, however, create a make-table query that copies existing records into a new table.

Access 97

Access 97 includes all the enhancements listed for Access 95, as well as some additional features. The list below describes the most significant of these new features.

- **Chart Wizard.** The improved Chart Wizard includes 20 different chart types. Several new chart types have been added: Cylinder, Pyramid, Cone, and Bubble.

- **Internet and Intranet Features.** Web applications can be created with the Publish to the Web Wizard. Datasheets, reports, or forms can be saved in an HTML format. Retrieve useful information from Microsoft online through the revised Help menu.

- **Hyperlink Data Type.** A new field data type has been added to create hyperlinks in datasheets, reports, and forms.

- **Performance.** The time it takes to display forms and reports has been reduced. The performance of embedded ActiveX controls has been improved. Software that isn't required for all databases, such as Visual Basic for Applications (VBA) isn't loaded until a database requiring that software is used, improving overall performance.

Additional enhancements and changes in Access 97 include the following:

- You have more control over PivotTable row and column headings than in previous versions of Access.

- When two digits are used for the century, dates entered from 1/1/30 through 12/31/99 are interpreted to mean 1930–1999. Dates entered from 1/1/00 through 12/31/29 are interpreted to mean 2000–2029.

Working with Databases from Earlier Versions of Access

You have three choices for working with databases created in earlier versions of Access. All three are available in Access 95 and Access 97:

- **Convert the database.** When you choose File, Open the Convert/Open Database dialog box appears, as shown in Figure 4.1. Select **1** Convert Database and the entire database is converted. Once converted, the database cannot be opened in, or converted back to, the previous version. It is wise to save a copy of your database *before* you convert it. Databases should not be converted until all users have been upgraded to the new version of Access.

- **Enable the database.** This is a good option when many people need to use the database but not all users have been upgraded to the newer version of Access. Choose File, Open and select **2** Open Database in the Convert/Open Database dialog box (see Figure 4.1). Enabling a database restricts some activities. Users in the newer version of Access can view database objects—tables, queries, forms, reports, macros, modules—and add, edit, or delete records but cannot modify the design of objects. To modify the design of an object or create a new object, the version of Access in which the database was created must be used.

- **Splitting the database.** The objects in a database are separated into two database files, creating a front-end/back-end application. Users who have been upgraded can take full advantage of the features in the new version, whereas those who have not yet been upgraded can still access the database in the earlier version. The "back-end" database file contains the tables. The "front-end" database file contains all other database objects and is linked to the tables in the back-end database. The back-end database file should contain the tables in the previous version of Access. The front-end database file should contain all the other objects in the new version of Access.

  You will need to use both the Database Splitter Wizard and the Linked Table Manager to accomplish this. The first step in the Database Splitter Wizard is shown in Figure 4.2. Both the Database Splitter Wizard and the Linked Table Manager are add-in programs in Access. The Linked Table Manager was known as the Attachment Manager in Access 2.0.

FIG. 4.1 ▶

Access 97—
Convert/Open
Database

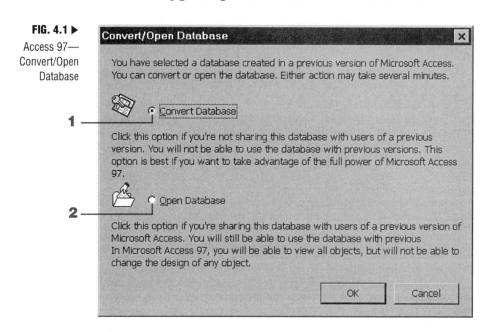

◀ FIG. 4.2

Access 95 and 97
Database Splitter

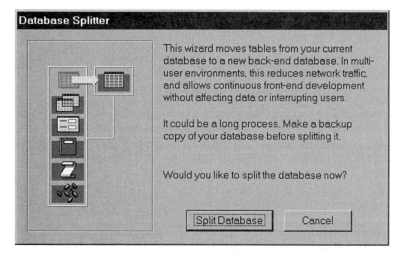

Saving Files in HTML Format (Access 97 Only)

New in Access 97 is the ability to save information from Access databases into a format that can be used on the Internet or your company's internal intranet. You can create online documents, such as a catalog of products your company sells. Tables, queries, forms, and reports can be converted to HTML (Hypertext Markup Language) format.

There are several ways to create files for the Web:

- **Exporting files to HTML format.** This is useful for creating a simple Web application, verifying the format and appearance of the object exported, or adding files to existing Web applications. You can also use an HTML template file, which contains HTML tags unique to Access 97 that enhance the appearance of your Web pages, and makes them easier to use.

- **Use the Publish to the Web Wizard.** The Publish to the Web Wizard assists you in converting your Access data into an HTML file. It outputs datasheets, forms, or reports to static or dynamic HTML format using HTML template files. It creates a home page and stores all files to a specified folder as a Web publication and copies the files to the Web server using the Web Publishing Wizard, and then saves a Web publication profile to use later.

To export a file in HTML format use the File, Save As/Export command. In the Save As dialog box, as shown in Figure 4.3, choose To an External File or Database. The Save *Object Name* In dialog box appears (see Figure 4.4). The specific **1** database object, a form named Products, is being exported not the entire database. Use **2** HTML for static file formats, or choose **3** Microsoft IIS 1-2 or Microsoft Active Server Pages for dynamic file format. To learn about the differences between static and dynamic format, type **html** in the Office Assistant search box and choose **About Static and Dynamic HTML format**.

To use the Publish to the Web Wizard choose File, Save as HTML. The first step in the wizard appears in Figure 4.5. Choose the objects from each of the **4** database tabs to include in the Web file, as shown in Figure 4.6.

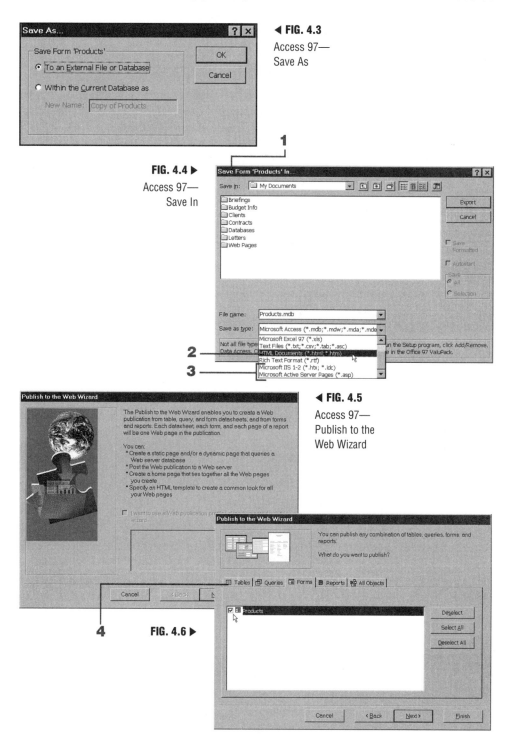

◀ **FIG. 4.3**
Access 97—
Save As

FIG. 4.4 ▶
Access 97—
Save In

◀ **FIG. 4.5**
Access 97—
Publish to the
Web Wizard

FIG. 4.6 ▶

Working in the Database Window

The layout of the database window in Access 95 and Access 97 has been modified (see Figure 4.7). Each database object type—tables, queries, forms, reports, macros, and modules—remains on its own tab. The **1** tabs now run across the top of the window instead of down the left side, as in Access 2.0. Additionally, the **2** command buttons have been moved from the top of the window to the right side. The command buttons are interactive; they change depending on the tab or object you have selected.

The database toolbar contains a set of icons that give you four options for viewing the database objects: **3** large icons, **4** small icons, **5** lists, and **6** details. Figure 4.8 shows the details for the database tables. The owner, description, date modified, date created, and object type are listed in the details. You can resize the columns of information or sort the list.

If you want to copy tables or queries into Excel or Word, you can drag the object icon from the Database window and drop it into a file in the other application. Likewise you can drag a group of cells from an Excel worksheet into the Database window to create a new table. Both applications must be open and visible to drag and drop. Right-click the Taskbar and choose one of the Tile options to display the application windows side by side.

> **TIP** To drag and drop database objects between two Access databases, open two copies of Access and arrange the windows.

Additionally, if you don't want an object displayed in the Database window, you can hide it by changing the object's properties. Right-click the object and choose Properties. Check Hidden under the section on Attributes.

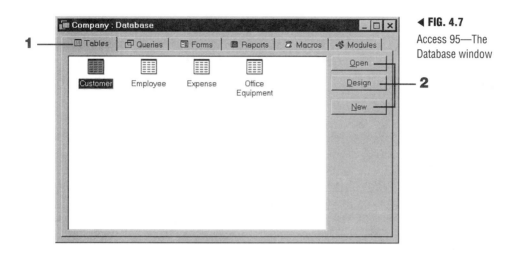

◀ **FIG. 4.7**

Access 95—The
Database window

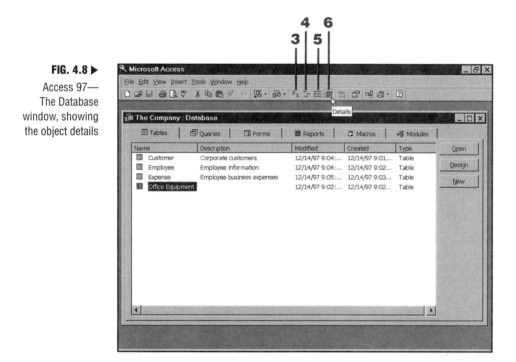

FIG. 4.8 ▶

Access 97—
The Database
window, showing
the object details

Databases

Creating New Databases Using the Built-in Templates

When you open Microsoft Access 95 or Access 97, the first screen you see gives you the option of creating a new blank database, creating a new database using the Database Wizard, or opening an existing database (see Figure 4.9).

Creating a database using a wizard is a new feature, available in both Access 95 and Access 97. You can quickly create an entire database in just a few simple steps. The database template wizard not only creates the database window, but creates tables, forms, queries, and even reports for the database. Figure 4.10 shows the list of templates in Access 97 on the **1** Databases tab in the New dialog box. The **2** General tab contains the Blank database template. The **3** Office 95 Templates tab contains a list of templates from Access 95, and appears only if you have upgraded from Access 95 to Access 97.

In Figure 4.10, the Inventory Control template is selected, and Figure 4.11 shows the first step in the Database Wizard. This step **4** explains what information the selected database, Inventory Control, is to store. Most of the wizards not only create the database, but create a **5** Switchboard to help you work with the database objects (see Figure 4.12). The **6** Database window is minimized in the lower-left corner of the Access window.

114

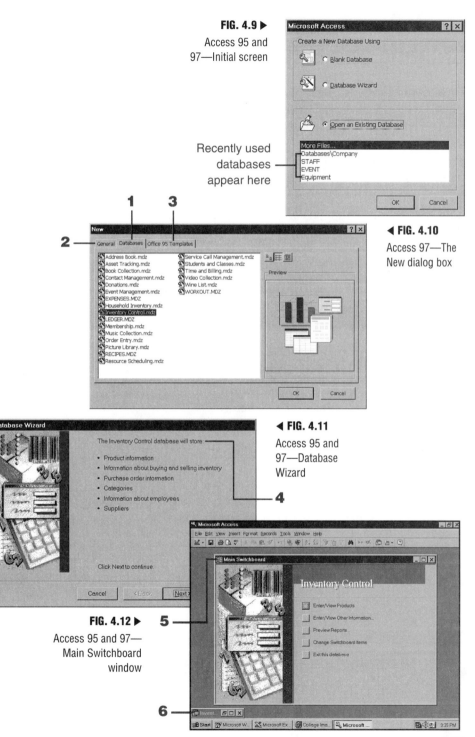

FIG. 4.9 ▶
Access 95 and
97—Initial screen

Recently used
databases
appear here

◀ FIG. 4.10
Access 97—The
New dialog box

◀ FIG. 4.11
Access 95 and
97—Database
Wizard

FIG. 4.12 ▶
Access 95 and 97—
Main Switchboard
window

115

Tables and Records
Creating and Editing Tables

Three options for creating tables in an Access 95 or Access 97 database are the Design View, Table Wizard, and Datasheet View. Using the Datasheet View to create a table was not an option in Access 2.0.

If you know the field names and field data types that you want to include in your database, the Design View (see Figure 4.13) is a quick way to create a table. You can specify **1** field properties and even **2** add a description to the field that appears on the Status bar when the field is selected in the Database View.

With the Table Wizard, you can use a wide variety of predefined table templates to create tables in Access. The table templates are **3** divided into two categories— Business and Personal (see Figure 4.14). The Business category contains traditional business tables—Customers, Employees, Orders, Suppliers, Invoices, Expenses, and others. The other category, though labeled Personal, contains tables appropriate for many types of business, as well as for personal home use. This category contains tables such as Guests, Plants, Wine Lists, Authors, Books, Recording Artists, and Investments.

The Table Wizard gives you the opportunity to select and rename the fields, set a primary key, and establish links to other tables. In the last step of the wizard, shown in Figure 4.15, you can **4** modify the field properties in the Design View, proceed directly to the **5** Datasheet View to enter data, or **6** have Access create an input form to enter the data into the table.

A new feature in Access 95 and 97 enables you to type data into the Datasheet View to have Access evaluate the data and automatically create the appropriate field types for you. The field names can be added or changed in Datasheet View at any time.

The Design View is used to modify the table structure, regardless of which method you used to create the table.

FIG. 4.13 ▶
Design View

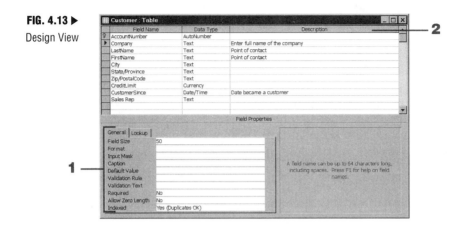

FIG. 4.14 ▶
Table Wizard—
Step one

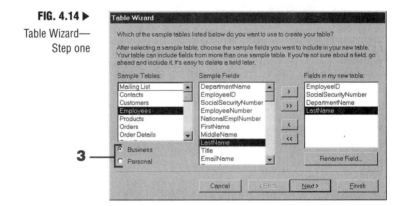

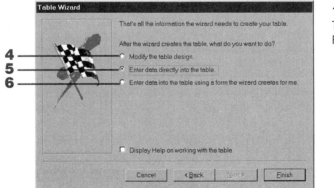

◀ FIG. 4.15
Table Wizard—
Final step

Changing the Table Format

Altering the appearance of a table in Access 95 or Access 97 gives greater flexibility. Cells can be given a raised or sunken look. Gridlines can be removed horizontally, vertically, or both. The gridline color can be changed. Data can be displayed in a different font, font style, and color. Fields (columns) can be inserted and renamed directly in the Datasheet View.

Several new field data types have been added to Microsoft Access 95 and 97. The Lookup data type uses a wizard to create a Lookup field that displays a list of values that are looked up in another table. Additionally, you can use the Lookup Wizard to create a field that displays a list of values that you define. The Hyperlink data type (available only in Access 97) is used to store a hyperlink to a file or to a Web site address. (Figure 4.16 shows examples of **1** Lookup and **2** Hyperlink type fields.)

Some fields have very specific ways they need to appear, such as Social Security Numbers and Phone Numbers. Included in the properties area of the Design View is the Input Mask property. When you click the property box, a Build button (ellipse) appears. This button starts the Input Mask Wizard (see Figure 4.17). The wizard has been improved so that you can customize and add to the list of input masks while running the wizard. The **3** Social Security Input Mask has been selected. When you click the **4** Edit List button, the **5** Customize Input Mask Wizard dialog box appears. You can either edit this input mask, or create a new mask by clicking the **6** New button.

2

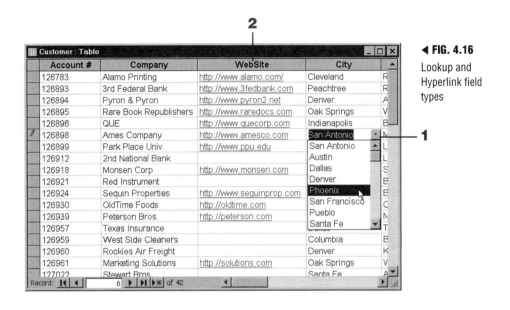

◀ FIG. 4.16

Lookup and
Hyperlink field
types

FIG. 4.17 ▶

Input Mask
Wizard

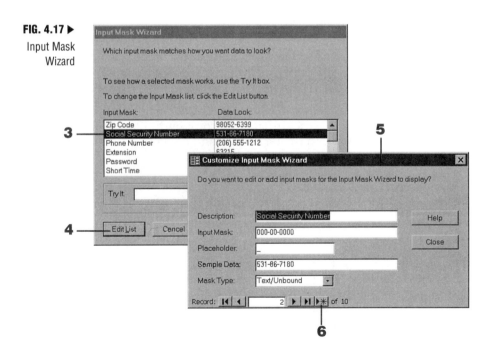

Tables and Records
Sorting and Filtering

Tables can contain large numbers of records. Two very useful commands that help you work with large amounts of data are Sort and Filter. The order in which records are added to a table is the order that they appear in the Datasheet View. At times, however, you want to see the records in a different order. Reorder records into ascending or descending order using the following methods:

- **Toolbar buttons.** The Ascending (A–Z) and Descending (Z–A) buttons on the toolbar. Sort the records, based on one field (column).

- **Shortcut menu.** Right-click the field in which you want to sort and choose Ascending or Descending.

- **Records menu.** The Sort command sorts based on one field (column). The Advanced Filter/Sort command sorts on multiple fields.

You can apply a filter to the records that display only those records that match your preferences. This enables you to see only those records in the table that you need. The following are several new ways to filter records in a table to create queries, forms, and reports. (Each of these methods is available in Access 95 and 97, unless otherwise noted.)

- **Filter By Selection.** Select the desired field and choose the Filter By Selection button on the toolbar.

- **Filter Excluding Selection.** Click a field that contains the data that you don't want to see, right-click, and choose Filter Excluding Selection.

- **Filter For.** (Available only in Access 97.) Right-click a field and type the criteria in the Filter For input line.

- **Filter By Form.** Choose the Filter By Form button on the toolbar and type the desired criteria into the form. The form contains drop-down lists from which you can select your criteria. Filters many fields.

- **Advanced Filter/Sort.** Formerly known as the Query By Example (QBE) grid, the Design Grid is used to perform complex sorts, filters, or combine sorting and filtering. Filters many fields.

Figure 4.18 shows the **1** Filter For input option on the shortcut menu and identifies some of the toolbar buttons used in sorting and filtering.

When you close a table that has been sorted or filtered, a prompt (shown in Figure 4.19) asks whether you want to save the table. If you save the table, the next time the table is opened the records appear in the order in which they were last saved. The filter is not applied but has been saved and can be applied by choosing Records, Apply Filter/Sort.

Even when a table is saved with a sort or filter, you can return the table to its previous state by choosing Records, Remove Filter/Sort.

120

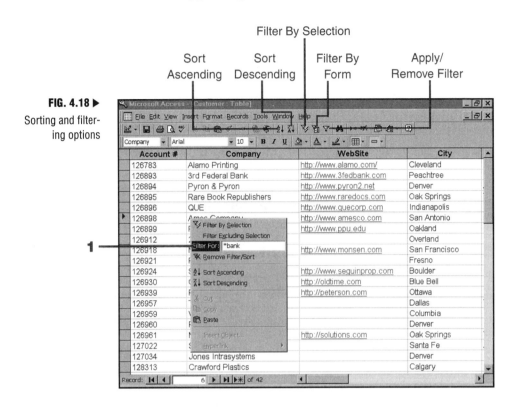

FIG. 4.18 ▶
Sorting and filter-
ing options

Filter By Selection

Sort   Sort   Filter By   Apply/
Ascending   Descending   Form   Remove Filter

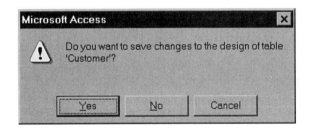

◀ FIG. 4.19
Save table dialog
box

Queries

Creating Queries Using the Wizards

Queries enable you to view, select, change, and analyze data in a variety of ways. Queries are frequently used as the source data for forms and reports. You can create queries in the Design View or using the Query Wizards.

The following types of queries can be created using the Query Wizards and are available in all versions of Access unless otherwise noted:

- **Simple Query Wizard.** A new type of query available only in Access 95 and Access 97 that is used to create a single or multi-table query. Can calculate sums, counts, or other types of totals. This type of query does not specify criteria—all records are included in the results.
- **Crosstab Query Wizard.** Used to summarize and analyze data; similar to a pivot table in Excel.
- **Find Duplicates Query Wizard.** Used to locate records with duplicate field values in a single table.
- **Find Unmatched Query Wizard.** Used to locate records in one table that have no related records in another table.

NOTE The Archive Query Wizard from Access 2.0 (Office 4.3) is no longer available. Create a Make-Table Query from the Design View to copy existing records into a new table.

To create a new query, activate the Queries tab in the Database window and choose New. Select from the list of four wizards.

Figure 4.20 shows the first step in the Simple Query Wizard. Several fields from the **1** Employee table are selected to be displayed in the query results. If you select a numeric or currency field, such as Salary or Rating, you have the option of creating summary calculations on that field.

Summary calculations work best when you pick two fields: one field to group records together and one field to summarize. In Figure 4.21, the **2** average rating grouped by department will be calculated and the employees in each department **3** will be counted. Figure 4.22 shows the result of the query. In the Design View, specify the number of decimals to display in the Avg of Rating column through the field properties.

FIG. 4.20 ▶

Simple Query
Wizard—Step
one

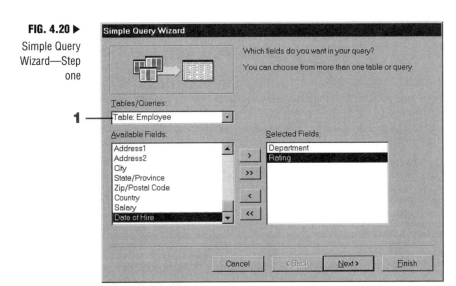

◀ FIG. 4.21

Simple Query
Wizard—Summary
options

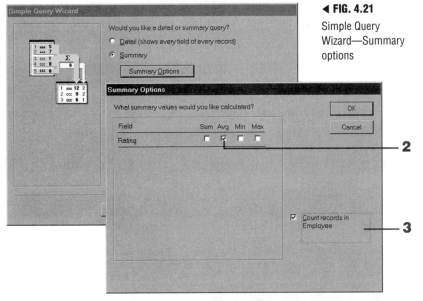

FIG. 4.22 ▶

Query results

Department	Avg Of Rating	Count Of Employee
Administration	2.19	28
Advertising	2.00	3
Customer Service	2.25	5
Human Resources	2.67	4
Inventory	2.20	5
Marketing	3.33	9
Sales	1.94	39

Record: I◀ ◀ 1 ▶ ▶I ▶* of 7

123

Queries

Creating Queries in the Design View

Although the Query Wizards are easy to use and prompt you for the information necessary to complete a query, the real power in querying comes in the Design View. The same query types available in Access 2.0 are still available in Access 95 and 97, the only difference is that a single button on the toolbar lists the query types in both Access 95 and 97 rather than individual buttons as in Access 2.0. The following is a list of query types in the Design View:

- **Select Query.** The default type of query created in the Design View. You can specify criteria, group and sort the output, and control field properties.

- **Crosstab Query.** Used to summarize and analyze data; similar to a pivot table in Excel.

- **Make-Table Query.** Creates a new table from the records retrieved in a query. Commonly used to create a backup for a table or for creating tables that are exported to another database in Access or to an Excel file.

- **Update Query.** Enables you to make global changes to data in existing tables.

- **Append Query.** A query that adds a group of records to an existing table. The data retrieved from the query is appended in the matching fields of the destination (or target) table. Any fields that do not occur in both the destination table and the retrieved records are ignored.

- **Delete Query.** A query that selects and deletes groups of records from a table based on the criteria you enter.

- **Parameter Query.** This type of query prompts you for information, such as a data range, before the query runs. The Parameter Query is not listed under the Query Type button. Instead they can be used in conjunction with other query types. They are created by typing in specific syntax in the criteria cell for a field, for example, **[Type the beginning date:]**.

Choose the Query Type button on the toolbar to select a different type of query. (Figure 4.23 shows a Select Query using multiple tables.)

NOTE   In Access 2.0, a join line automatically displayed between tables in the query Design View that contained fields with the same name and data type. In Access 95 and 97, you can disable this feature by choosing Tools, Options and selecting the Tables/Queries tab. Remove the check in the Enable AutoJoin option.

124

FIG. 4.23 ▶

A query in the
Design View

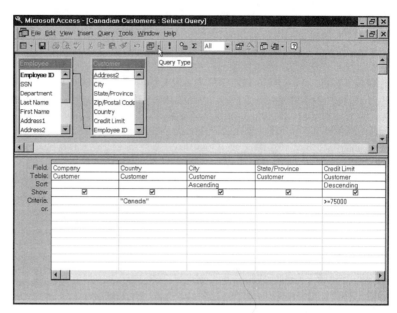

Editing Queries

Editing queries is done in the Design View, regardless of how the query was originally created. The editing options available in Access 95 and Access 97 are identical to those available in Access 2.0. You can add calculated fields, include built-in functions in your queries, and specify field properties. The key to retrieving what you want from a database and displaying it in the desired format lies in the criteria and other parameters that you specify.

Calculations are frequently used in queries. You can create a calculation that shows a new salary if you give all employees a 10 percent raise. In an empty column in the design grid, click the Field row. **1** Type in **New Salary: Salary*1.1**. (Figures 4.24 and 4.25 show the query in the Design View and the results of the query in the Datasheet View.)

Functions are used in calculations to return a value. Two frequently used functions are NULL and DATE().The NULL function locates records that contain blank or empty values. The DATE() function returns the current date. If today is April 5, 1998, the DATE() function displays 4/5/98, tomorrow it would display 4/6/98.

Sometimes the result displays a large number of decimals, such as 3.245612. To display the result as a whole number or with a specific number of decimals, right-click the field in the Design View and choose Properties. Use Format and Decimal to specify the properties you prefer.

You can use queries to perform quick statistical calculations, such as a sum of employee salaries or counting the number of employees in each department. To create these types of calculations, add the Total row to the design grid by choosing the Totals button on the toolbar. The key to accurate statistical calculations is to use one field as the group and *only* those fields on which you intend to perform calculations. (Figure 4.26 shows the Design View with the Total row added; **2** Department is the group field.)

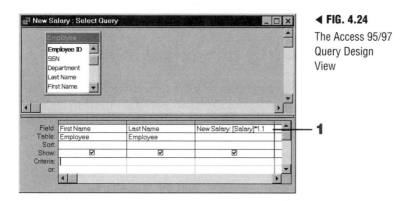

◀ FIG. 4.24

The Access 95/97
Query Design
View

1

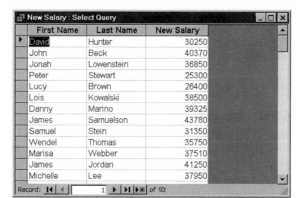

◀ FIG. 4.25

The Access 95/97
Query Datasheet
View

FIG. 4.26 ▶

Statistical calcu-
lations in a query

2

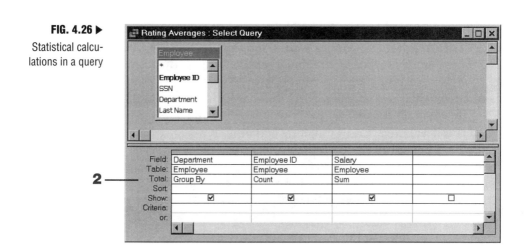

Reports

Creating Reports Using the Wizards

Reports provide the most powerful means of organizing data that is pulled from a table or query and printed or published online. You can group and sort data; add graphics, like company logos; and calculate subtotals, grand totals, and other statistics. A variety of formatting options enable you to enhance your reports.

Reports can be created in several ways—using built-in wizards, through a button on the toolbar, or from scratch in the Design View. Many of the types of reports you created in Access 2.0 are available in Access 95 and 97. Some types have been expanded, consolidated, or renamed. The following table illustrates the changes made to the report wizards.

Access 2.0 Wizards	Access 95/97 Wizards
Single-Column Wizard	Included in the Report Wizard
Group/Totals Wizard	Included in the Report Wizard
Mailing Label Wizard	Renamed Label Wizard
Summary Wizard	Included in the Report Wizard
Tabular Wizard	Included in the Report Wizard
AutoReport Wizard	Expanded to include two types: Columnar and Tabular
MS Word Mail Merge	Now available through the Tools, Office Links command

The report wizards in Access 95 and 97 are

- **AutoReport: Columnar and AutoReport: Tabular.** Automatically creates a simple columnar or tabular report, using all the records in the table or query.
- **Chart Wizard.** A new report wizard available in Access 95 and Access 97. Creates a chart based on the data in a table or query.
- **Label Wizard.** Creates mailing and other types of labels using standard Avery or custom labels. Called the Mailing Label Wizard in Access 2.0.
- **Report Wizard.** Creates a comprehensive report based on a query or table. The wizard prompts you for information on orientation, layout, font style and color, groups, sort order, and summary options.

Figure 4.27 shows a multitable report that was created using the Report Wizard. Reports are modified in the Design View.

FIG. 4.27 ▶

Preview of an
Access 97 report

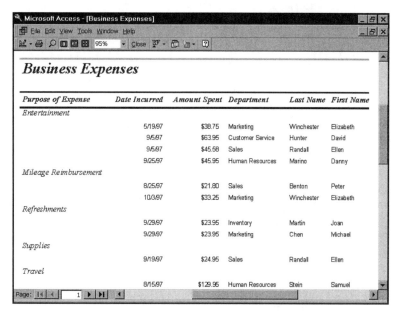

Creating Reports in the Design View

Whether you are working in Access 2.0, Access 95, or Access 97, the use of the Design View to create reports is similar. The report is divided into sections, toolbars provide quick ways to edit or insert objects in the report, and you can preview your changes as you go along.

With regard to creating or editing a report, the biggest difference in the Design View between Access 2.0 and Access 95/97 is the location of the menu commands. Many of the commands have been moved to other menus. For example, the command to add the Report Header and Footer section is located under the View menu in Access 95/97 (see Figure 4.28) instead of the Format menu, as in Access 2.0. A new menu in Access 95 and 97, Insert, includes options to add charts, pictures, and page numbers to your reports. Some of these options are available in Access 2.0 but were more difficult to insert.

Another difference between these three versions of Access is the toolbars and toolbar buttons available in the Design View. In addition to the **1** Report Design and **2** Toolbox toolbars available in Access 2.0, the **3** Formatting Toolbar also appears in the Design View in both Access 95 and 97. Some of the buttons, such as Bold and Italics, which were on the Report Design toolbar in Access 2.0, are now on the Formatting toolbar.

Although you can create a report entirely from scratch in the Design View, it can be very time-consuming. A better approach is to start with an AutoReport, which at least places the fields (and their corresponding labels) in the report for you. You can then use the Design Views to format the layout, add titles, form groups, create calculations, and add graphics.

To create an AutoReport that displays data from multiple tables or includes specific fields, use a query. (Figure 4.29 shows the result of the AutoReport based on the Customer table in the Design View.)

Use the buttons on the Report Design toolbar to activate the **4** Toolbox toolbar, **5** form groups and sort the records, **6** format the layout, **7** change field properties, and **8** build formulas and expressions. Use the buttons on the **9** Toolbox toolbar to add labels and calculated fields and insert graphics. (Figure 4.29 shows the dialog box where you indicate the sorting and grouping options that you want to add to a report.)

FIG. 4.28 ▶
The Access 97
Design View

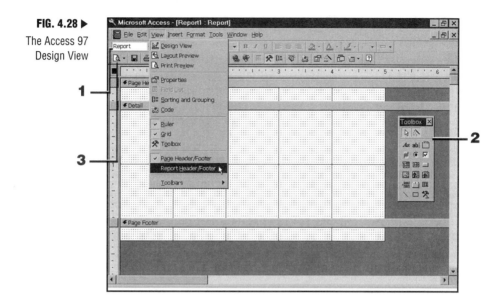

◀ FIG. 4.29
The Access 97
AutoReport
results

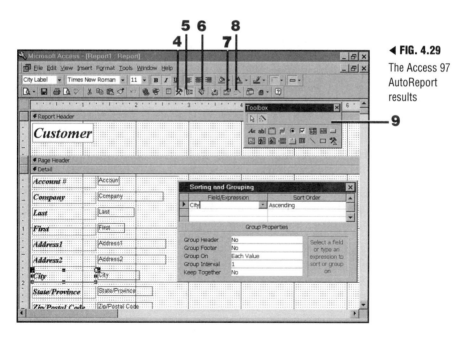

Formatting and Editing Reports

Regardless of which version of Access you are using or how the report is created, you use the Design View to edit and enhance the report. The report Design View is divided into sections: Page Header, Detail, and Page Footer. Other sections such as Report Header or Report Footer can be added. These sections are used to display a title or logo to the first page of the report or a report summary at the end of the report. (Figure 4.30 shows **1** a logo in the Report Header section.)

Group Header and Group Footer sections are added to group records by a common field value and create subtotal calculations by group. (Figure 4.30 has a Group Header and Group Footer listing the employees by department and **2** calculating the sum of the salaries. Additionally, **3** a technique known as concatenation is used to display the employee's first and last names together, as if they were one field. The **4** number of years each employee has been with the company is being calculated.)

Many improvements have been made in Access 95 and 97 to the formats that can be added to your reports:

- **AutoFormat.** Apply an autoformat to completely change the look of your report. (Figure 4.31 shows the AutoFormat dialog box.) AutoFormats include **5** predefined fonts, colors, and borders. You can **6** modify the predefined formats or customize your own.

- **Formatting Toolbar.** The new Formatting toolbar, available in Access 95 and 97, enables you to quickly format the object on a report using formatting buttons you're familiar with from Word and Excel.

- **Special effects.** Additional settings for the Special Effect property include chiseled, etched, or shadowed.

- **Format Painter.** Copies formats such as font, color, and size from one label or text box to another using the Format Painter button introduced in Access 95.

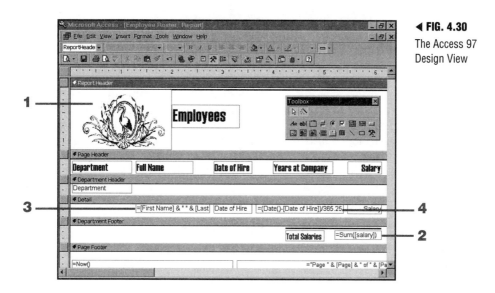

◀ FIG. 4.30
The Access 97
Design View

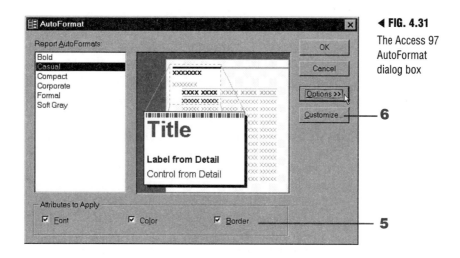

◀ FIG. 4.31
The Access 97
AutoFormat
dialog box

Forms

Creating Forms Using the Wizards

Forms are a great alternative to entering data directly into a table. A variety of formatting options can be used to enhance your forms, and forms can be created in several ways—using built-in wizards, through a button on the toolbar, or from scratch in the Design View. Many of the types of forms you can create in Access 2.0 are available in Access 95 and 97. Some types have been expanded, consolidated, or renamed. The following table illustrates the changes made to the form wizards.

Access 2.0 Wizards	Access 95/97 Wizards
Single-Column Wizard	Included in the Form Wizard
Tabular Wizard	Included in the Form Wizard
Graph Wizard	Renamed Chart Wizard
Main/Subform Wizard	Included in the Form Wizard
AutoForm Wizard	Expanded to include three types: Columnar, Tabular, and Datasheet

The types of forms you can create using wizards in Access 95 and 97 are:

- **AutoForm: Columnar, AutoForm: Tabular, and AutoForm: Datasheet.** Automatically creates a simple columnar, tabular, or datasheet form, using all the records in the table or query.
- **Chart Wizard.** Creates a chart based on the data in a table or query. Available in Access 95 and 97. Significantly enhanced in Access 97. Called the Graph Wizard in Access 2.0.
- **PivotTable Wizard.** New in Access 95 and 97. Used to summarize large amounts of data. You specify the calculation and formats for the PivotTable. A PivotTable is like a crosstab query. You must have Microsoft Excel installed to use this wizard.
- **Form Wizard.** Creates a comprehensive form based on a query or table. You no longer have to create a query in order to produce a form based on data from multiple tables. From within the wizard, you can select fields from more than one table. The wizard prompts you for information on layout and style.

The Form Wizard also makes it easy to create a form with a subform. Subforms are used to show data from tables with a one-to-many relationship. (Figure 4.32 shows a form with **1** a subform that was created using the Form Wizard.)

FIG. 4.32 ▶

An Access 97
form

1 ——

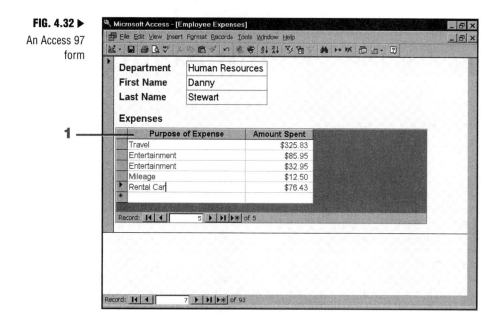

Forms

Creating Forms in the Design View

The way in which you use the Design View to create forms is similar whether you are working in Access 2.0, Access 95, or Access 97. You can display the Form View to see the changes you make as you go along.

With regard to creating or editing a form, the biggest difference between Access 2.0 and Access 95/97 is the location of the menu commands. Many of the commands have been moved to other menus. For example, the command to change the Tab Order is located under the View menu in Access 95/97 instead of the Edit menu as in Access 2.0. A new menu in Access 95 and 97, Insert, includes options to add charts, pictures, and page numbers to your forms (see Figure 4.33). Some of these options are available in Access 2.0 but were more difficult to insert.

Another difference between these three versions of Access is the toolbars and toolbar buttons available in the Design View. In addition to the **1** Form Design and **2** Toolbox toolbars available in Access 2.0, the **3** Formatting Toolbar also appears in the Design View in both Access 95 and 97. Some of the buttons, such as Bold and Italics, which were on the Form Design toolbar in Access 2.0, are now on the Formatting toolbar.

Creating a form entirely from scratch in the Design View can be very time-consuming. Instead, start with an AutoForm, which places the fields (and their corresponding labels) in the form for you. You can then use the Design View to format the layout, rearrange the fields, and add controls and graphics. (Figure 4.34 shows the result of the AutoForm based on the Orders table in the Design View.)

Use the buttons on the Form Design toolbar to activate the **4** Toolbox toolbar, **5** format the layout, and **6** change field properties. Use the buttons on the Toolbox toolbar to **7** add labels, **8** controls, and **9** graphics. (Figure 4.34 shows the Properties dialog box for the Price field.)

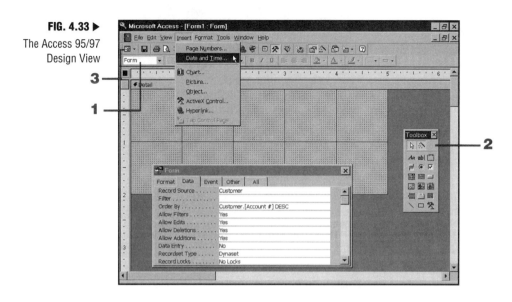

FIG. 4.33 ▶

The Access 95/97 Design View

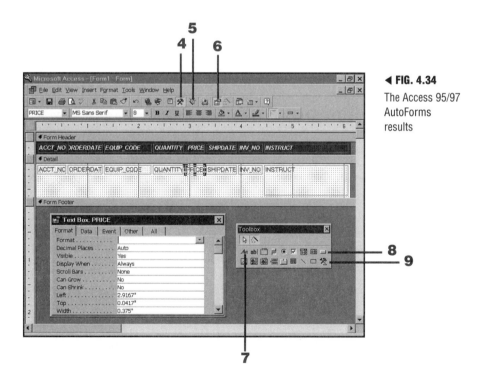

◀ FIG. 4.34

The Access 95/97 AutoForms results

Formatting and Editing Forms

Regardless of which version of Access you are using or how the form is created, you use the Design View to edit and enhance the form. The form Design View is divided into sections: Form Header, Detail, and Form Footer. Additionally, the Page Header and Page Footer sections can be added by choosing View, Page Header/Footer. These sections are only displayed on printed forms; they do not appear on screen.

Many improvements have been made in Access 95 and 97 to the formats that can be added to your forms:

- **AutoFormat.** Apply an autoformat to completely change the look of your form. AutoFormats include predefined fonts, colors, and borders. You can modify the predefined formats or customize your own.

- **Formatting Toolbar.** The new Formatting toolbar, available in Access 95 and 97, enables you to quickly format the object on a form, using formatting buttons you're familiar with from Word and Excel. A chiseled, etched, or shadowed appearance can be set for the controls on a form using the Special Effects button.

- **Format Painter.** Copy formats such as font, color, and size from one label or text box to another using the Format Painter button on the toolbar.

The List Box and Combo Box Wizards have been improved and made more efficient. You can create a list box or combo box that finds a related record on a form, or you can filter the records in another list box or combo box. You can create a screen tip on a form that appears when the mouse pointer is placed over a control by modifying the control's properties. (Figure 4.35 shows an example of **1** a screen tip entered for the OrderDate control in the **2** Properties dialog box.)

FIG. 4.35 ▶

A form in the
Access 97 Design
View

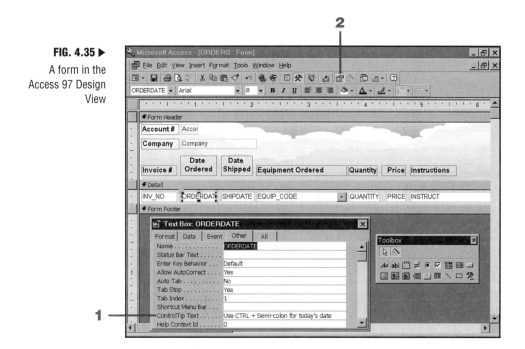

Builders

Creating Expressions

An expression is a type of calculation that returns a result. Expressions are used in queries, reports, and forms and can be used in all versions of Access. To create an expression, you can type it from scratch or use the Expression Builder (see Figure 4.36). The Expression Builder consists of several sections:

- **1 The Expression Box.** Displays the expression you are building
- **2 Operator Buttons.** Operators commonly used in expressions
- **3 Left Box.** Lists the table, query, form, and report database objects, built-in and user-defined functions, constants, operators, and common expressions
- **4 Middle Box.** Lists the elements for the folder you select in the left box
- **5 Right Box.** Lists the values for the elements you select in the left and middle boxes

The Expression Box in Figure 4.36 shows an expression that concatenates the First Name and Last Name fields to display the data from these two fields as if it were one field. The ampersand (&) or plus (+) is used to display text fields as if they were a single entry. Quotes are used to create a space or add text that you type in to an expression. Another common expression, which uses concatenation, is to merge several address fields:

=[Address] & ", " & [City] & " " & [State] & " " & [ZipCode]

Expressions are also used to perform calculations.

When these expressions are used in a report, precede each expression with the equal (=) symbol, for example **= [OrderDate] - [ShippedDate]**. When used to display a calculation in a query, precede each expression with a name followed by a colon (:), for example **Processing : [Orderdate] - [ShippedDate]**. The name property must be unique; don't use the name of one of the fields used in the expression.

FIG. 4.36 ▶

The Expression
Builder

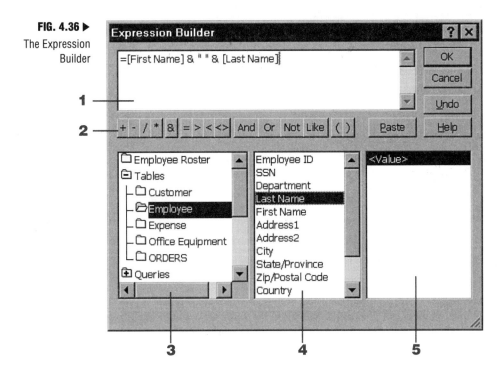

Creating Functions

Like expressions, functions return a value and are used in conjunction with expressions. Functions are available in all versions of Access and can be used in queries, reports, forms, property settings, and Visual Basic statements. You can use functions in the expressions you type from scratch or in the Expression Builder. Examples of commonly used functions include the following:

Function	Example	Description
Trim()	Trim([Price])	Displays the value of the Price field, removing any leading or trailing spaces.
Avg()	Avg([Quantity])	Averages the values in the Quantity field.
Count()	Count([EmployeeID])	Counts the number of records in the EmployeeID field.
Sum()	Sum([Quantity]*[Price])	Totals the result of calculating the amount due per item, for all records.

Another popular function is IIf(). The IIf function is comprised of three components: an expression, what to do if the expression is true, and what to do if the expression is false. An example of an IIf function is:

IIf([Quantity] < 10,[Quantity]*[Price],[Quantity]*([Price]*.9)

If the value in the Quantity field is less than 10, then multiply the Quantity times the Price; otherwise (the Quantity is equal to or greater than 10), multiply the Quantity times 90% of the Price—giving the buyer a 10% discount.

The IsNull() function is often used with the IIf function to avoid problems in calculations where a record may have an empty field, for example:
=IIf(IsNull([OrderDate] - [ShippedDate]), "Missing a date", [OrderDate] - [ShippedDate]).The IIf function is used to display the message "Missing a date" if the result of subtracting ShippedDate from OrderDate is Null; otherwise, it displays the result of the subtraction.

Figure 4.37 shows a report in the Report Design View. The records are **1** grouped by Department and functions are being used to calculate **2** the number of years each employee has been with the company and **3** the total salaries paid by each department.

FIG. 4.37 ▶

The Access 97
Report Design
View

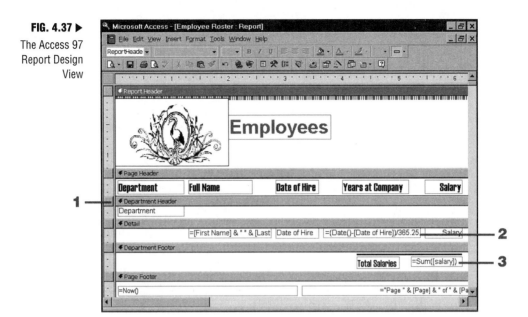

Importing and Exporting

Importing Data from Excel

When an Excel spreadsheet no longer provides the capabilities needed to manipulate your data, several new options from which you can choose enable you to import data from Excel into Access. In Access 2.0, the File, Import command is used to bring data in from Excel. In Access 95 and 97, choose File, Get External Data and select the Excel workbook to import into Access. The new Import Spreadsheet Wizard assists you in selecting the correct field delimiters and field data types and with setting a primary key. Figure 4.38 shows the first step in the Import Spreadsheet Wizard. Indicate whether your Excel list **1** contains a row of headings that are to be used as field names. Figure 4.39 shows another step in the wizard where you can **2** add or change the field name, **3** index the field, **4** select the data type, or **5** indicate the field should not be imported.

On the last step of the Import Spreadsheet Wizard, you are provided an option to run another wizard to analyze the data that you are importing. When you select this option, the new Table Analyzer Wizard starts immediately after your data is imported. This wizard helps to make your database more efficient by indicating when to split a large table into two or more smaller tables. (In Figure 4.40, the Table Analyzer Wizard has identified duplicate entries in your list and **6** shows you a generic sample of the problem.) Additionally, it can illustrate why duplicate data can **7** waste space and **8** lead to mistakes.

FIG. 4.38 ▶

Import
Spreadsheet
Wizard

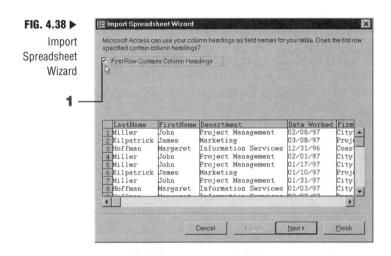

◀ FIG. 4.39

Import
Spreadsheet
Wizard—Field
Options

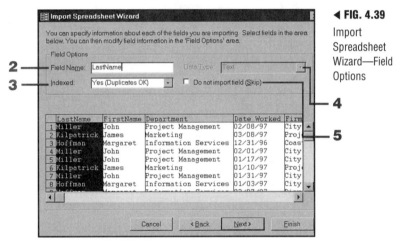

◀ FIG. 4.40

Table Analyzer
Wizard

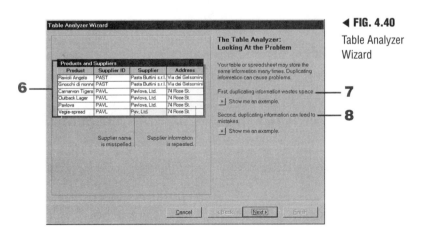

Importing and Exporting
Exporting Data to Excel

There are options from which you can choose to export data from Access into Excel. In Access 2.0, the File, Export command is used to copy data to Excel. In Access 95 and 97, when you choose File, Save As/Export command, the Save As dialog box appears (see Figure 4.41) asking whether the Access table is to be saved as an external file to export it to Excel, Word, or another database file. To save the table in Excel, choose To an External File or Database. The Save In dialog box appears (shown in Figure 4.42). You complete several items in this dialog box:

■ Choose the **1** folder in which to save the file.

■ Enter a **2** file name for the new file.

■ Select the appropriate **3** file type. Access can save the table in several Excel versions.

■ Determine whether you want the **4** formatting associated with the Access file to carry over into Excel.

After you have completed the Save In dialog box, click the **5** Export button to save the data in the Excel format.

A New feature in Access 95 and 97 enables you to drag and drop data from Access to Excel. By arranging the Excel and Access program windows on the screen, you can select a table or query from the Access Database window and drag the object into an Excel workbook. Specific data from an Access form or datasheet can also be dragged into Excel.

Data can also be copied from Access and pasted into Excel. A new feature in Access 95 and 97 retains formats such as font, alignment, and number formatting when data is copied into Excel.

FIG. 4.41 ▶

The Save As
dialog box

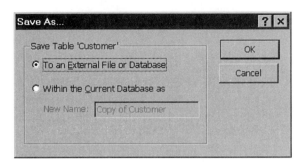

FIG. 4.42 ▶

The Save In
dialog box

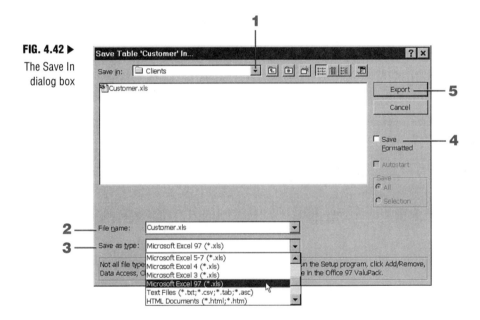

Upgrading to Microsoft PowerPoint 95 and PowerPoint 97

A number of enhancements have been made to both PowerPoint 95 and 97, making PowerPoint the best application for creating slide show presentations. The features introduced in this chapter are grouped by topic:

- **What's New.** Learn about the new features that have been added to PowerPoint.

- **Managing Files.** Convert files created in previous versions of PowerPoint to your current version of PowerPoint. Discover the built-in content templates, which lay out the order and scope of topics that should be discussed for frequently used types of presentations. Choose from among dozens of design templates for professionally designed presentations.

- **Working with Charts.** Learn about the improved features for creating charts. Animate your charts for a powerful presentation impact.

- **Slide Show Techniques.** Take advantage of the slide show shortcut menu and keyboard shortcuts to move around while giving a presentation. Add animation effects to charts, clip art, and text. Create branches and hyperlinks to other presentations or Internet Web sites.

- **Slide Show Features.** Enhance your presentations with multimedia clips, including pictures, sound, and video. Create summary slides quickly.

- **Presentation Alternatives.** New features enable you to take minutes and assign action items while running a slide show. Presentations can be run over an intranet or the Internet.

What's New

PowerPoint 95

PowerPoint 95 has a number of new and enhanced features. The following list describes many of these new features:

- **Multimedia.** Include sound and video clips in your presentations. The Office 95 CD contains a number of clips to get you started.

- **Animation.** You can animate the slide title, bullet text, clip art, and drawn objects in PowerPoint 95. Many of the animation effects are similar to the slide transition effects. The new Animation Effects toolbar makes it easy to access the animation commands.

- **Object Fill Options.** Many enhancements have been made to the Fill options that you can apply to your presentation. In the past, when you applied a gradient fill you selected one color and had the option of seeing that color transition into black or white. The gradient fill now includes an option to select 2 colors, for example blue transitioning into green. Textured fills such as marble, cloth, wood, and granite are also available.

- **Improved Color Schemes.** Each design template comes with a default color scheme and alternative color schemes. You can also customize your own scheme and save it with a design template to use in future presentations.

- **Meeting Minder.** Add new notes to your notes pages, take minutes during your presentation, and create a list of action items using the Meeting Minder.

- **Presentation Conferencing.** Participants no longer have to be in the same room to view a slide show. The Presentation Conference Wizard walks you through the steps to run a slide show over a network.

- **Presentations on the road.** The Pack and Go Wizard packs or compresses all necessary files, including multimedia and other linked files so that you can take your presentation on the road or send it to someone else.

Additional enhancements and minor changes in PowerPoint 95 include the following:

- In addition to checking your spelling, PowerPoint now checks your punctuation and capitalization with the Style Checker.

- You can now undo multiple actions. The default is 20 of your last actions, with a maximum of 150.

- In addition to a Slide Master, PowerPoint 95 now has a separate master just for Title slides instead of an Outline Master.

- New tools are available while running a slide show. A shortcut menu is now available which includes the Slide Navigator, a tool for moving around in your presentation, and the Slide Meter shows the timing of your presentation compared to the times you rehearsed.

■ Notes pages can now show multiple miniature images of slides and you can print multiple pages of notes using the Write Up command.

PowerPoint 97

PowerPoint 97 includes all the enhancements listed for PowerPoint 95, as well as some additional features. The list below describes the most significant of these new features.

Enhanced Charting. One of the most significant improvements in Office 97 is the charting program. Many new chart types have been added, including cylinders, pyramids, bubbles, and pie of pie. Charts can be animated, displaying one series or category at a time. Fill effects include pictures, as well as texture and gradient fills. You can add a data table to your charts instead of a legend.

Programming in PowerPoint. You can use Visual Basic for Applications to create custom features, dialog boxes, and add-ins. Create presentations that enable the user to select from a list, check a box, and other ActiveX controls.

Office Art. Common to all Office 97 programs, the revised Drawing toolbar includes many new and enhanced features. A large list of AutoShapes has been added, along with 3D effects and shadows.

Hyperlinks. Create links documents in other programs or to sites on the Internet. You can also use this feature to link to slides in the same presentation or to other presentations.

PowerPoint 97 has some additional enhancements and changes:

■ You can create several versions of a presentation, tailored to different audiences using the Custom Shows command.

■ Design self-running, interactive slide shows for conventions, conferences, and trade shows.

■ Using the new Action Settings command to set interactive settings for an object is easier. You can assign two different actions to an object.

■ Additional animation effects and multimedia clips are available in the ValuPack folder on the Office 97 CD. Use the new PowerPoint Central feature to locate multimedia clips on the Office 97 CD or on the Internet.

■ You can locate and preview specific slides in a presentation and insert these slides in other presentations using the Slide Finder command.

■ Colleagues can add comments to slides without changing the content of the slides with the Presentation Comments command.

Converting Files from Older Versions of PowerPoint

You can display a file created in an earlier version of PowerPoint by simply opening the file in your current version of PowerPoint. To convert a file from an earlier
version of PowerPoint to a newer version, you must save the file.

- **PowerPoint 95.** PowerPoint 4.0 files are displayed as Read-Only files in
  PowerPoint 95. You must use the File, Save As command and select the **1**
  Presentations (*.ppt) file type when saving the file to convert it to
  PowerPoint 95 (see Figure 5.1). Use the **2** PowerPoint 4.0 (*.ppt) file type to
  save it back in that version.

- **PowerPoint 97.** PowerPoint 4.0 and 95 files are displayed as if they were
  created in PowerPoint 97, with full Read-Write capabilities. When you
  attempt to save a file that was created in an earlier version of PowerPoint,
  the dialog box displayed in Figure 5.2 appears. You have the choice of saving
  the file as a PowerPoint 97 file or keeping the file in its current version.

If you have created a file in PowerPoint 95, you have to save the file in a
PowerPoint 4.0 format before you can open the file in PowerPoint 4.0. Any fea-
tures unique to PowerPoint 95, such as long filenames, are not displayed in
PowerPoint 4.0. A filename such as **Annual Conference.ppt** is changed to
Annual~1.ppt when saved in the PowerPoint 4.0 format.

When you save a presentation file in PowerPoint 97, the default file type is **3**
Presentation (*.ppt), which saves it as a PowerPoint 97 file. Use the **4** Save As
Type drop-down to see a list of file type alternatives. You can also save it as a **5**
PowerPoint 95 & 97 Presentation, **6** a PowerPoint 95 presentation, or a **7**
PowerPoint 4.0 presentation. These formats enable you to open the file in these
versions of PowerPoint. (Figure 5.3 shows an example of the Save As dialog box in
PowerPoint 97 and the choices you have for changing the file type.)

FIG. 5.1 ▶

PowerPoint 95—
File Save dialog
box

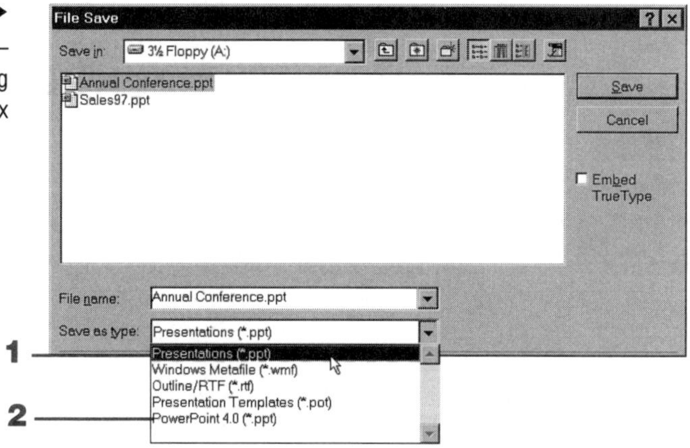

◀ FIG. 5.2

PowerPoint 97
overwrite dialog
box

FIG. 5.3 ▶

PowerPoint 97
Save As dialog
box

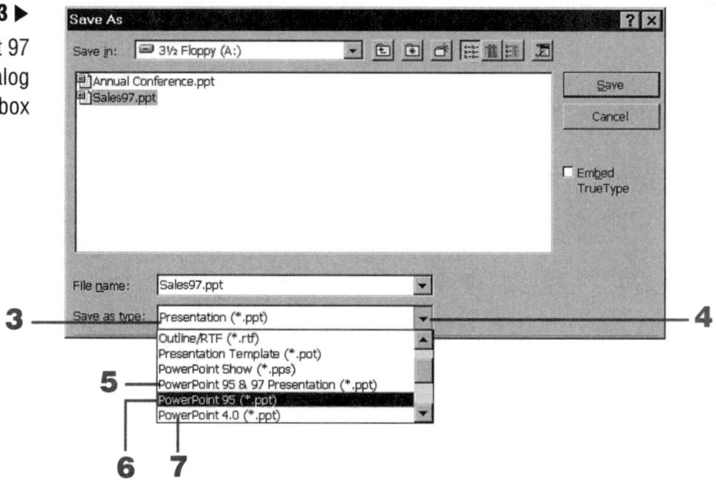

Creating New Files Using the Built-in Templates

The content and design templates are the two template types in PowerPoint.

- **Content templates.** These are predesigned presentations that focus on a particular goal. For example, content templates are used for recommending a strategy, reporting progress, or communicating bad news. These templates propose the type of information you should include in a presentation and the flow of the topics to achieve the desired results. Additionally, they include a background design to complement the topic being presented.

- **Design templates.** These are predesigned presentations that focus solely on the appearance of the presentation and have content. PowerPoint has design templates appropriate for professional settings as well as more whimsical templates for informal presentations.

PowerPoint 4.0 contains 6 content templates and 55 design templates. PowerPoint 95 and PowerPoint 97 have added new content and design templates, though not all the templates in PowerPoint 97 are installed automatically. Look in the ValuPack folder on the Office 97 CD for more templates.

You can create a new presentation using a content or design template from the initial screen in PowerPoint (shown in Figure 5.4). The **1** AutoContent Wizard is used for content templates. The **2** Template option is used to choose a design template. (Figure 5.5 shows the roadmap in the AutoContent Wizard. You can work your way through each step, or select a specific step to enter the wizard.)

You can also choose the File, New command in either PowerPoint 95 or 97 to create a presentation based on a template. A dialog box with several tabs appears (shown in Figure 5.6). The default Blank Presentation template is on the **3** General tab. The **4** Presentation Designs tab contains a list of the predesigned design templates. The **5** Presentations tab contains a list of the content templates.

PowerPoint 97 has a **6** Web Pages templates tab. If you have upgraded from PowerPoint 95, the **7** Office 95 Templates are listed on their own tab. A **8** preview of the selected template appears on the right side of the dialog box (see Figure 5.6).

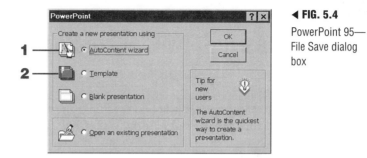

◄ FIG. 5.4

PowerPoint 95—
File Save dialog
box

FIG. 5.5 ►

PowerPoint 97—
AutoContent
Wizard

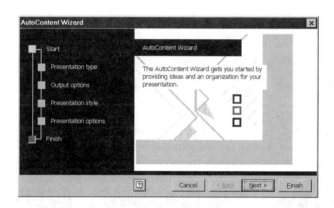

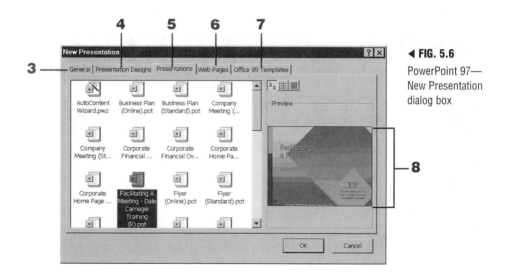

◄ FIG. 5.6

PowerPoint 97—
New Presentation
dialog box

Managing Files

Saving Files in HTML Format (PowerPoint 97 Only)

New in PowerPoint 97 is the capability to save your presentations in a format that can be used on the Internet or your company's intranet. This format is known as Hypertext Markup Language or HTML. A wizard assists you in converting your PowerPoint presentations to HTML files.

> **NOTE** PowerPoint comes with some templates that help you design your presentation for online viewing.

You can convert a presentation to Web pages by saving your file using the File, Save as HTML command. The Internet Assistant guides you through the steps for creating the necessary files used in the Internet or intranet Web server. You can include animations from your presentation, use frames, select the background and hyperlink colors, and select different button styles.

Each presentation slide is turned into an individual HTML page. Any existing hyperlinks are converted to HTML format, and actions that you assigned through the Action Settings command are translated into equivalent HTML commands and settings. All the necessary files are then saved to a new folder that you specify. Internet Assistant quickly converts your presentation into a series of linked Web pages, ready to publish on the Web.

Figure 5.7 shows the first step in the Internet Assistant Wizard. A roadmap appears on the left. The **1** Office Assistant provides useful information throughout the conversion process. Figure 5.8 shows the step for selecting the graphic type. A **2** description of the selected option appears in the Office Assistant pop-up. Figure 5.9 shows the step for choosing background and hyperlink colors.

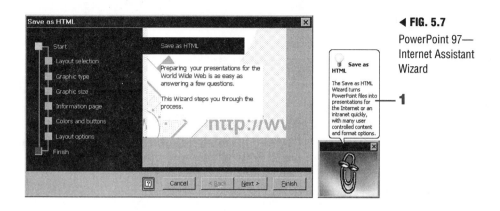

◀ FIG. 5.7

PowerPoint 97—
Internet Assistant
Wizard

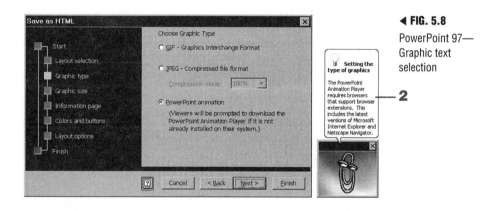

◀ FIG. 5.8

PowerPoint 97—
Graphic text
selection

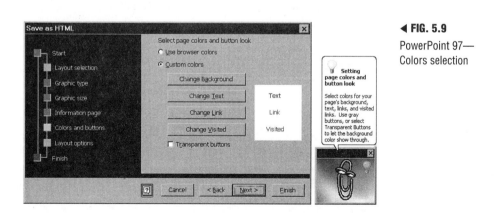

◀ FIG. 5.9

PowerPoint 97—
Colors selection

Creating and Modifying Charts

When you create a chart in PowerPoint, a separate program used by all Microsoft applications for creating graphs, Microsoft Graph, is automatically launched. Many improvements have been made in Microsoft Graph, especially in Office 97.

There were 10 basic chart types in PowerPoint 4.0. In addition to the 10 previously available, 4 new chart types have been included in PowerPoint 95 and PowerPoint 97. The **1** Bubble is a new chart type, similar to the scatter chart. The **2** Cylinder, Cone, and Pyramid chart types are variations of the column and bar charts. The Pie of Pie and Bar of Pie are variations of the Pie chart used to further break out specific components of a wedge of the original pie. (Figure 5.10 shows the Chart Type dialog box, illustrating the new pie chart variations.)

In addition to the standard chart types, 20 predesigned custom chart types have been included in both PowerPoint 95 and 97. You find special types like Combination charts and Logarithmic charts under the custom types as well as some of the standard chart types that have been modified with colorful backgrounds or shading. Click the **3** Custom Types tab in the Chart Type dialog box.

Other improvements to charts in PowerPoint 97 include the following:

- Revised menu and toolbar choices.
- Data tables are now available in charts (see Figure 5.11).
- The number of data points plotted per series increases from 4,000 to 32,000, which is particularly useful in line and scatter charts to show more accurate trends.
- New formatting options, such as using pictures or texture for fills and scaling marker size.
- Chart tips available when you rest the mouse pointer over a chart object.
- Improved display of text in charts, including text rotation.

To change any of the components of a chart in either PowerPoint 95 or 97, choose Chart, Chart Options. (Figure 5.11 shows the Chart Options dialog box.) A 3D Column chart is displayed with a **4** new feature, a data table, instead of a legend.

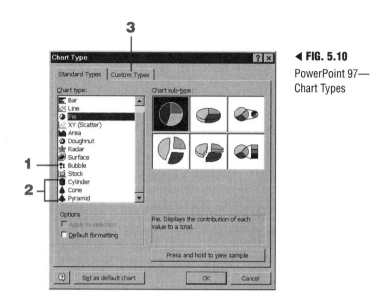

◀ **FIG. 5.10**

PowerPoint 97—
Chart Types

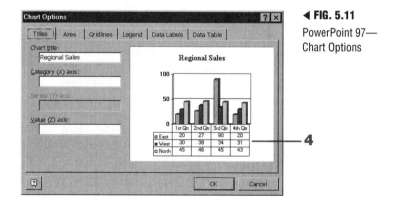

◀ **FIG. 5.11**

PowerPoint 97—
Chart Options

Chart Animation

In PowerPoint 95, you can use animation effects similar to the transition effects you can apply to slides or the build effects you can attach to bulleted text. Transition effects are discussed later in this chapter.

Using animation effects, the chart can fly from bottom-right or "box out." One important enhancement made to PowerPoint 97 is the capability to build components of a chart. Figure 5.14 shows a column chart that compares Revenue and Expenses for each quarter of this year. The x-axis displays Quarter 1, Quarter 2, and so on. One series of columns represents revenue and another series of columns shows expenses. You can build the chart one quarter at a time, comparing revenue and expenses for each quarter, or you can display all the revenue columns at one time.

You can also build a pie chart, one piece at a time until the entire pie is constructed. In fact, you can use chart animation with any of the chart types in PowerPoint. Individual data points on a chart can be animated, too.

In PowerPoint 95, use the Animation Settings command on the Tools menu to add transition and sound effects. (Figure 5.12 shows the Animation Settings dialog box in PowerPoint 95.) You can select **1** how the chart is to appear on the screen and **2** what sound you want to play as the chart appears.

PowerPoint 97 provides two ways to apply animation in your slide show. Predesigned animation effects can be applied to a chart quickly by choosing Slide Show, Preset Animation. Custom chart animation is available through Slide Show, Custom Animation. You must be in the Slide View to customize chart animation. Figure 5.13 shows the animation and sound options on the Chart Effects tab of the Custom Animation dialog box. Each category on the x-axis appears using the Box Out transition effect; no sound plays during the animation. (Figure 5.14 illustrates a column chart being animated by category—Quarter).

Organization charts can be animated with timing, transitions, and sound. Unlike bar charts and pie charts, the components of organizational charts cannot be built, they appear all at once.

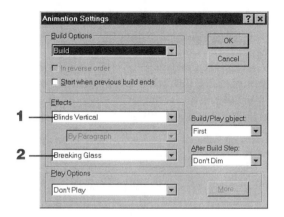

◀ **FIG. 5.12**
PowerPoint 95—
Animation
Settings

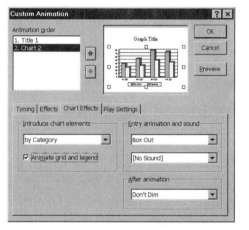

◀ **FIG. 5.13**
PowerPoint 97—
Chart Effects tab

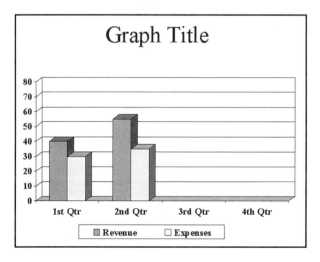

◀ **FIG. 5.14**
PowerPoint 97—
Animated
categories

Navigating in a Slide Show

You can preview your presentation from any view in PowerPoint. To preview your presentation from the current slide, click the Slide Show button located in the lower-left corner of your screen. To preview from the first slide use the Slide Show, View Show command.

You can use either the keyboard or the mouse to navigate while running a slide show presentation. Most shortcuts are available in all versions of PowerPoint; a few new shortcuts have been added to PowerPoint 97. The following table lists shortcuts.

Navigation Options	Keyboard or Mouse Shortcut
Next slide	N, ENTER, right arrow, or the SPACEBAR (or click the primary mouse)
Previous slide	P, left arrow, or BACKSPACE
Go to slide #	# + ENTER
Black screen	B
White screen	W
Stop or restart	S
End a slide show	ESC
Erase annotations	E
Return to the first slide	Both mouse buttons for two seconds
Change the pointer to a pen	CTRL + P (PowerPoint 97 Only)
Change the pen to a pointer	CTRL + A (PowerPoint 97 Only)
Hide the pointer and button temporarily	A or CTRL + H (PowerPoint 97 Only)
Hide the pointer and button always	CTRL + L (PowerPoint 97 Only)
Display the shortcut menu	SHIFT+ F10 or right-click (PowerPoint 97 Only)

> **NOTE** In all versions of PowerPoint, you can press F1 during a slide show to see a list of keyboard and mouse shortcut controls.

You can also use your mouse to navigate in a slide show. In PowerPoint 4.0 and PowerPoint 95, you can right-click the mouse to see the previous slide. PowerPoint 97 uses this button to provide a shortcut menu with a number of useful slide show options. (Figure 5.15 shows the PowerPoint 97 slide show shortcut menu.)

FIG. 5.15 ▶
PowerPoint 97—
Shortcut menu
Animation
Settings

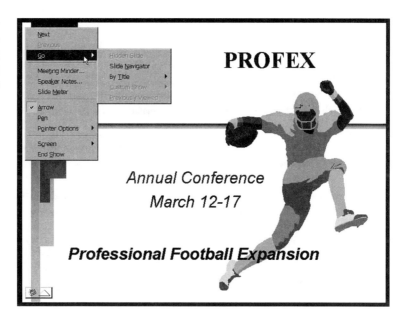

Slide Show Techniques
Animation Effects

Animation, or a build, is a special effect you apply to your slide objects indicating when and how the objects appear on a slide during a slide show. In PowerPoint 4.0, you can only build (animate) slides with bulleted text. Each bullet appears one at a time, to build the topics on a slide. In both PowerPoint 95 and 97, not only can you animate bulleted lists, but virtually any object on the slide. Additionally, in PowerPoint 97, you can animate parts of a chart as well. The terms, animation and build, are used interchangeably.

In PowerPoint 95, the commands for animating slide objects are located under the Tools menu. The Build Slide Text command enables you to animate your bulleted text. The Animation Settings command can be used to animate other objects such as slide titles and charts as well as bulleted text. (Figure 5.16 shows the Animation Settings dialog box.) Some of the options are only available for specific types of objects.

In PowerPoint 97, you can select Preset Animation or Custom Animation from the Slide Show menu. Preset Animation effects are designed to help you quickly enhance your presentation. Many of the Preset Animation effects include both transitions and sound. Custom Animation, on the other hand, provides a wide range of options from which you can select. (Figure 5.17 shows the Custom Animation dialog box in PowerPoint 97.)

At the top of the dialog box is an area labeled **1** Animation Order and **2** a miniature of your current slide. The animation options are divided among the four tabs—Timing, Effects, Chart Effects, and Play Settings. In Figure 5.17, three objects are shown on the slide; the title, the bulleted text, and the pie chart. The numbers listed after each object is the order in which it was created. **3** The chart is being animated. The title and text appear immediately when this slide is displayed. When **4** the mouse is clicked, the chart appears. As you apply animation settings, use the **5** Preview button to show (and hear) the animation effects on the miniature slide in the upper-right corner of the dialog box.

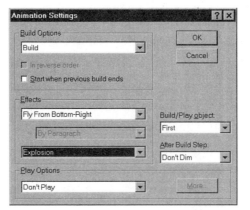

◀ FIG. 5.16
PowerPoint 95—
Animation
Settings

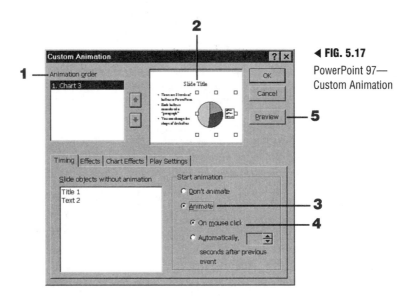

◀ FIG. 5.17
PowerPoint 97—
Custom Animation

Slide Show Techniques

Branches and Hyperlinks

Branches are supplementary presentations that you create to provide additional information on a topic in your main presentation. The branch presentation is linked to an object in your main presentation. When you activate that object, the branch presentation begins. After the branch presentation is concluded, the main presentation continues.

In PowerPoint 7.0, setting up a branch to another PowerPoint presentation is a two-step process. You must first insert an icon in the slide from which you want to branch and then establish exactly what should happen when the other presentation is displayed. To insert the icon, choose Insert, Object. The Insert Object dialog box displays (shown in Figure 5.18). Using the **1** Link and **2** Display As Icon settings, an icon will be inserted into your active slide. After you have inserted the icon, choose Tools, Interactive Settings to display the Interactive Settings dialog box (see Figure 5.19). To have the other presentation start when you click the inserted icon, choose Show from the **3** Object Action drop-down list.

The Interactive Settings dialog box also includes options to go to another slide in the current presentation, run another program, and play a sound. To accomplish this, select an object in your slide to use as a button to perform the action. You can use the slide title, an object you have drawn, or even clip art as your button. After you have the button selected, choose the desired option in the Interactive Settings dialog box.

When you branch to another presentation, you automatically return to the slide in your main presentation from which you activated the branch. When you go to a slide within the current presentation, use a keyboard shortcut, the Slide Navigator, or make another button with which to return to the other slide.

In PowerPoint 97, the capability to link to other items has been expanded. The term *hyperlink* is used to encompass all the types of links you can create, including branches. You can also use hyperlinks to go to a specific location on your company's intranet or the Internet, a new feature in PowerPoint 97.

To create a hyperlink in PowerPoint 97, select the object you want to use as the button with which to activate the link, and then choose Slide Show, Action Settings. You can use the slide title, an object you have drawn, or clip art as your button.

You have a choice of activating a hyperlink in a slide by resting the mouse pointer over the hyperlink or by clicking the hyperlink. Select either the Mouse Click or Mouse Over tab in the Action Settings dialog box (see Figure 5.20). The options on these tabs are exactly the same. From this dialog box, you can create a hyperlink, start a program, run a macro, or play a sound. (In Figure 5.20 a **4** hyperlink has been created to the slide that contains the title **Agenda** in the current presentation.)

FIG. 5.18 ▶
PowerPoint 95—
Insert Object

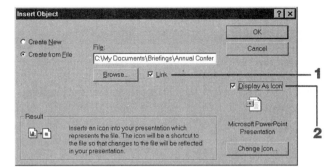

FIG. 5.19 ▶
PowerPoint 95—
Interactive
Settings

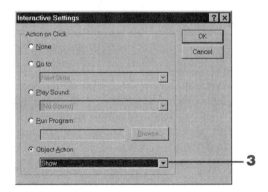

FIG. 5.20 ▶
PowerPoint 97—
Action Settings

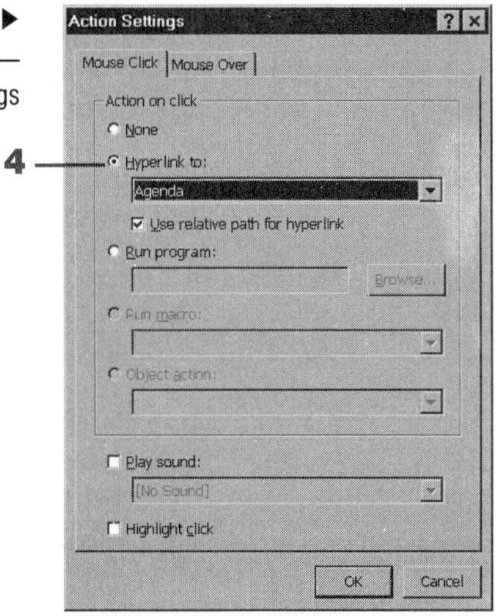

Slide Show Techniques

Action Settings (PowerPoint 97 Only)

Hyperlinks are one of several types of actions that can be used in slide show presentations. An action can be attached to any object in a PowerPoint slide—text, charts, tables, clip art, or drawn objects. After you've determined which object to use as the button for the action, you need to specify the action you want taken.

You have three options when working with actions:

- Perform the action when you click the object.
- Perform the action when you rest the mouse pointer on the object.
- Perform two separate actions, one when you click the object and another when you rest the mouse pointer on the object.

Choose Slide Show, Action Settings to select the action options you want to apply to an object.

Figure 5.21 shows the Action Settings dialog box, with the Mouse Click tab selected. When the object in the slide is clicked during a slide show, a **1** hyperlink to the Macmillan Publishing Web site at **http://www.mcp.com** is activated. Additionally, **2** the beginning of Beethoven's 9th Symphony plays. Sound files are located on the Office 97 CD in **clipart/mmedia**.

You can create a hyperlink to another slide in the active presentation, another PowerPoint presentation, another Windows file such as an Excel worksheet, or to either an address on the Internet or an intranet using a URL (Uniform Resource Locator).

Figure 5.22 shows the Mouse Over tab of the Action Settings dialog box. When the mouse is positioned over the slide object, **3** another program is launched. Additional options include **4** running a macro and setting **5** actions options.

FIG. 5.21 ▶
PowerPoint 97—
Mouse Click tab

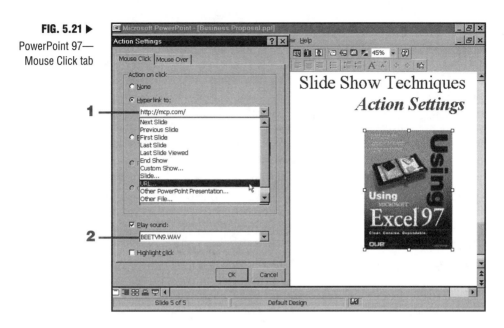

FIG. 5.22 ▶
PowerPoint 97—
Mouse Over tab

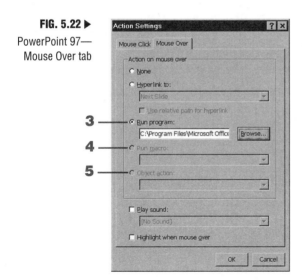

Slide Show Techniques

Action Buttons (PowerPoint 97 Only)

PowerPoint 97 comes with a set of built-in three-dimensional buttons that can be used for hyperlinks. These buttons consist of commonly used interactive buttons and appear depressed when clicked during a slide show presentation. They are particularly useful with kiosk-type presentations, which enable the user to play media clips or move forward or backward in a presentation.

To create one of these built-in action buttons, click AutoShapes on the Drawing toolbar. Point to Action Buttons and select the button you want. (Figure 5.23 shows the **1** Home button selected.) You can also select the Action Buttons from the Slide Show menu. Figure 5.24 identifies each of the 12 built-in action buttons. The default action setting is listed in parentheses.

After you have selected the action button, position the mouse pointer where you want the button to appear on the slide and click once. The button is created and the Action Settings dialog box appears. You can use the default action setting for the button, or choose a new setting. (See the Action Settings topic on the previous page for more information on using this dialog box.)

The buttons can be resized and the appearance altered. Figure 5.25 shows three action buttons. The **2** first button is Custom and has been modified to display a gradient fill. The **3** second button is Information and has a denim textured fill. The **4** third button is Help and has a water droplets textured fill. A **5** hyperlink to the Microsoft Web site has been attached to this button.

To change the button fill, select the button and choose Format, AutoShape.

FIG. 5.23 ▶
PowerPoint 97—
Action buttons

FIG. 5.24 ▶
PowerPoint 97—
Action buttons
identified

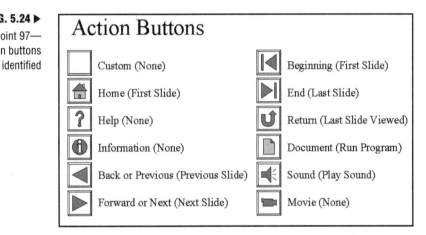

FIG. 5.25 ▶
PowerPoint 97—
Customized
action buttons

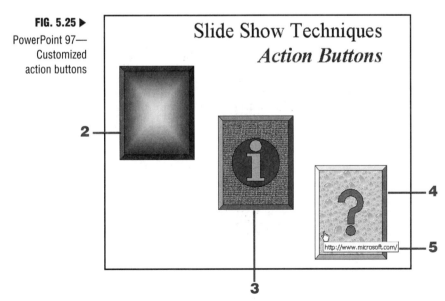

Slide Show Techniques
Slide Color Schemes

Every design template in PowerPoint contains a default color scheme consisting of eight coordinated colors. In addition to the default color scheme, a new feature available in PowerPoint 95 and 97 includes alternative color schemes for each design template. The default and alternative color schemes in a template comprise the Standard color schemes for that template. (Figure 5.26 shows an example of the Standard color schemes for a design template. The **1** default color scheme is the first scheme on the top row. To access the Color Scheme dialog box choose Format, Slide Color Scheme.) The Standard color schemes for each template are professionally designed with coordinated colors so that you can apply one color scheme to a group of slides and another color scheme to another group of slides in the same presentation. Additionally, you can customize a specific color in a scheme or create your own color schemes. You choose what you want to customize in the **2** Custom tab of the Slide Color Scheme dialog box. (Figure 5.27 shows the Color Scheme Custom tab in PowerPoint 97. The Custom tab in PowerPoint 95 contains all the options shown in Figure 5.27, but is laid out slightly differently.)

Each of the eight colors that comprise a color scheme is listed on the Custom tab. A **3** preview of the color scheme appears as a miniature slide on the lower-right corner of the dialog box. Select the color that you want to change and click the Change Color button. From the Background Color dialog box (shown in Figure 5.28) you have the choice of selecting a Standard color, white, shades of gray, and black. You can also design your own color by clicking the Custom tab in the Background Color dialog box. (Figure 5.29 shows the Custom tab.)

The easiest way to customize a color is to use the **4** Red, Green, and Blue options at the bottom of the dialog box. The highest number available is 255. Using this number in red, green, or blue creates the sharpest color. (Figure 5.29 shows Blue with 255 and zero color in Red and Green.)

You can add a custom scheme to the list of standard schemes for a specific presentation. To use the custom color scheme in other presentations, you can save your presentation as a custom design template.

FIG. 5.26 ▶
PowerPoint 97—
Standard tab

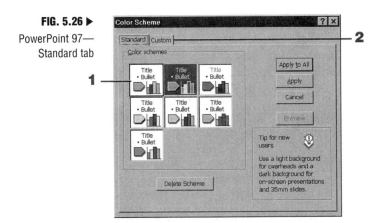

FIG. 5.27 ▶
PowerPoint 97—
Custom tab

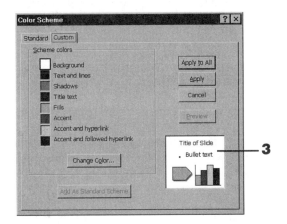

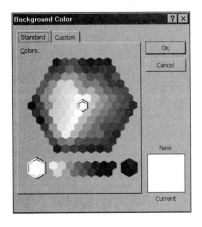

◀ FIG. 5.28
PowerPoint 97—
Background
Color, Standard
tab

FIG. 5.29 ▶
PowerPoint 97—
Background
Color, Custom tab

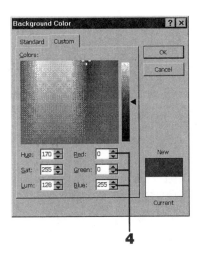

173

Adding Pictures, Video, and Sound to Presentations

Using multimedia clips can greatly enhance your PowerPoint presentations. You can add photos, music, sounds, and video clips to your PowerPoint 95 or PowerPoint 97 presentation through the Insert menu. Some clips, like sounds and video, can be attached to other objects as hyperlinks. To change how the clip starts or to add a hyperlink to the clip in PowerPoint 95, choose Tools, Interactive Settings. In PowerPoint 97, choose Slide Show, Action Settings.

Figure 5.30 shows the Pictures tab of the Microsoft Clip Gallery dialog box. The **1** Sunflower photograph is selected. In PowerPoint 97, most of the pictures, sounds, and videos are stored on the Microsoft Office 97 CD. The **2** Import Clips button will create a pointer to these images on the CD and will display a thumbnail in your Clip Art Gallery.

Figure 5.31 shows the Sounds tab of the Microsoft Clip Gallery dialog box. **3** Beethoven's 9th Symphony is selected. If you have Internet access, you can locate additional multimedia clips by selecting the **4** Web icon in the Clip Gallery dialog box. Use the **5** Play button to hear a sound or see a video.

Figure 5.32 shows the Videos tab of the Microsoft Clip Gallery dialog box. The **6** Basket video is selected. A **7** description of the selected multimedia object is listed at the bottom of the dialog box. Click the **8** Clip Properties button to learn more about a clip.

When you insert a multimedia clip in a slide, an image representing the clip is inserted in your slide.

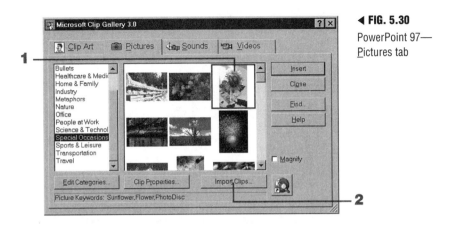

◄ FIG. 5.30
PowerPoint 97—
Pictures tab

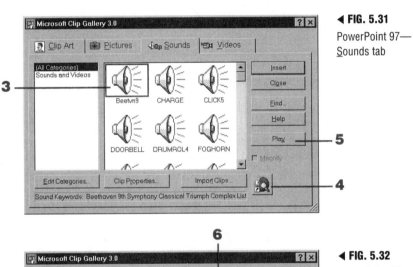

◄ FIG. 5.31
PowerPoint 97—
Sounds tab

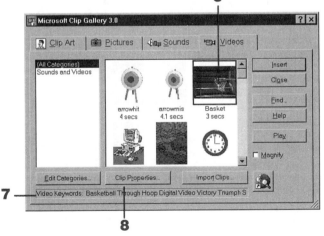

◄ FIG. 5.32
PowerPoint 97—
Videos tab

Summary Slides (PowerPoint 97 Only)

Most people follow these three principles when making presentations:

- Tell them what you are going to tell them.
- Tell them.
- Tell them what you told them.

With the first and last bullets above, it is useful to have a slide summarizing the topics. A new feature in PowerPoint 97 enables you to create a summary slide listing the topics being discussed for the entire presentation or just a section. You can also use the Summary Slide feature to recap what was presented in the slide show. Summary slides are created in the Slide Sorter or Outline Views.

Figure 5.33 shows a series of slides in the Slide Sorter View. The titles from the selected slides are to be used as bullets in the summary slide. Figure 5.34 shows the result when you create a summary slide. The **1** new slide is inserted in front of the first slide in the selected group but can be moved or copied to the end of the presentation as a wrap-up slide.

To create the summary slide, select the slides, which you want to be summarized (hold the Shift key while selecting multiple slides). Then click the **2** Summary Slide button, located on the Slide Sorter toolbar. The Summary Slide button is also available on the Outline toolbar when you are in the Outline View.

You can create a hyperlink from a bulleted item in the summary slide to the detail slide, which facilitates moving around in the presentation. To create the hyperlink, you must be in the Slide View. Select the bulleted item in the summary slide and choose Slide Show, Action Settings. Select the Hyperlink option and choose Slide. Select the specific slide to which you want to link from the list that appears. (Figure 5.35 shows the Action Settings dialog box with a **3** hyperlink to the Profit Sharing slide.)

FIG. 5.33 ▶
PowerPoint 97—
Slide Sorter View

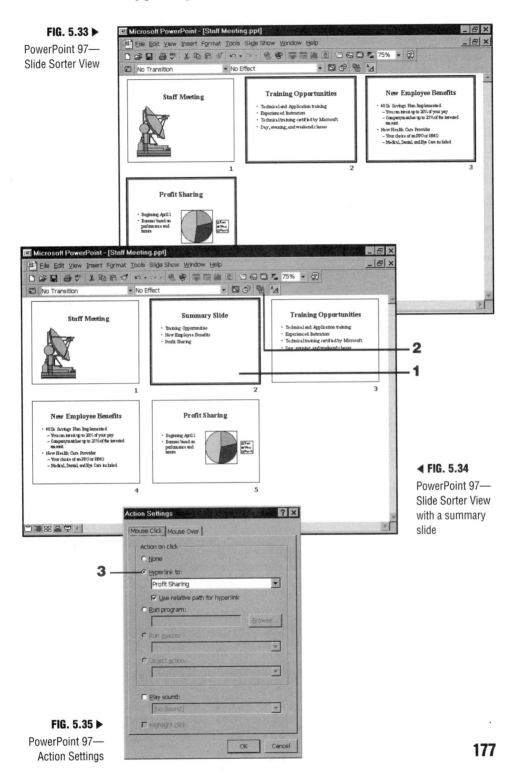

◀ FIG. 5.34
PowerPoint 97—
Slide Sorter View
with a summary
slide

FIG. 5.35 ▶
PowerPoint 97—
Action Settings

177

Expanding Slides (PowerPoint 97 Only)

Periodically you may create slides that contain more data than can reasonably fit on one slide, or main bullets may need further elaboration. The new Expand Slide command in PowerPoint 97 breaks a crowded slide into multiple slides. Each top-level bullet point (and the corresponding subbullets) are placed on its own slide, making for a cleaner presentation of the topics. The Expand Slide command works only with slides, which contain bulleted lists.

Figure 5.36 depicts a slide that contains more information than can be reasonably viewed on a single slide. The **1** text is bleeding off the slide. From the Slide Sorter View, select the Tools, Expand Slide command. Figure 5.37 shows the result of using the Expand Slide command. Each main bullet on the **2** original slide becomes the title for the **3** new slide. Subbullets from the original slide are promoted to main bullets on the new slide.

The new slides are inserted after the original slide. You can delete the original slide or remove the subbullets and turn it into a summary slide.

The Expand Slides command can be used in the other views. If you expand a slide in the Slide or Notes Page View, a prompt appears asking whether you want to see the new slides in the Outline or Slide Sorter View.

FIG. 5.36 ▶
PowerPoint 97—
A cluttered bullet
slide

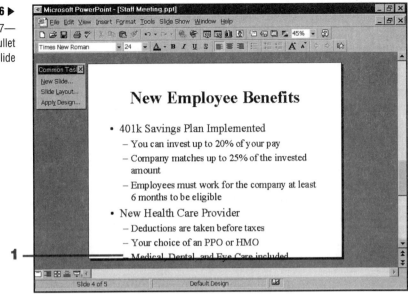

FIG. 5.37 ▶
PowerPoint 97—
Newly inserted
slides

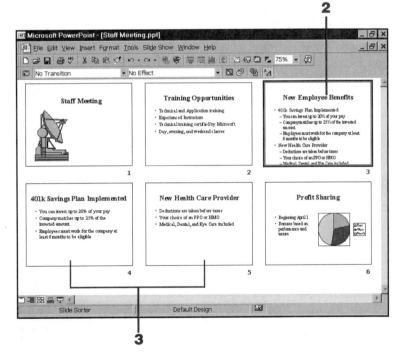

Presentation Alternatives
Meeting Minder

The Meeting Minder was first introduced in PowerPoint 95 as a way to view your slide notes, create minutes, and generate a list of action items while you are running a slide show presentation. PowerPoint 97 continues to use the Meeting Minder, with several improvements. To access the Meeting Minder, right-click the slide and choose Meeting Minder from the shortcut menu. (The PowerPoint 95 shortcut menu is shown in Figure 5.38 and the Meeting Minder dialog box is shown in Figure 5.39.) Each tab in the Meeting Minder dialog box is a blank page in which you enter the information you want. Any notes you have added in the Notes Pages View appears on the Notes Pages tab in the Meeting Minder dialog box (see Figure 5.39). Click **1** the Export button to send minutes and action items to a file in Microsoft Word or add the meeting minutes to your Notes pages.

The PowerPoint 97 shortcut menu and Meeting Minder dialog box are shown in Figure 5.40. Just as in PowerPoint 95, the Meeting Minutes tab is a blank page for you to enter the minutes. Figure 5.41 shows the Action Items tab. This tab has been formatted to make entering in action items easier and includes a place for **2** a description, **3** the person assigned to the action, and **4** the due date.

Click **5** the Export button to send minutes and action items to a file in Microsoft Word or post the action items to Microsoft Outlook. Click **6** the Schedule button to schedule a meeting in Microsoft Outlook (provided that you have installed Outlook). In PowerPoint 97, you can still view the notes entered in the Notes Pages View through **7** the Speaker Notes option on the shortcut menu.

Action items entered in either PowerPoint 95 or PowerPoint 97 appear on a new slide at the end of your presentation. This slide is automatically generated by PowerPoint. (Figure 5.41 shows an example of this slide.)

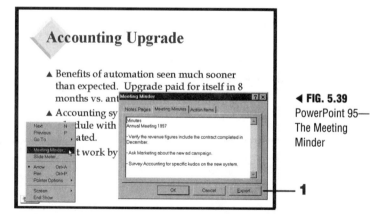

FIG. 5.38 ▶
PowerPoint 95—
Slide Show short-
cut menu

◀ FIG. 5.39
PowerPoint 95—
The Meeting
Minder

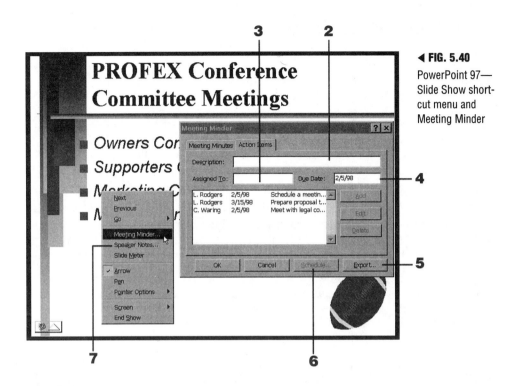

◀ FIG. 5.40
PowerPoint 97—
Slide Show short-
cut menu and
Meeting Minder

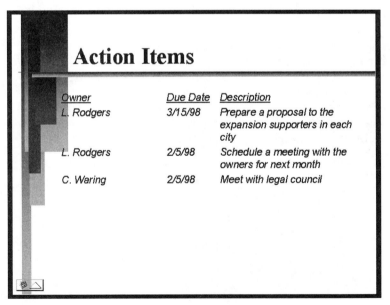

◀ FIG. 5.41
PowerPoint 97—
The Action Items
slide is automati-
cally added to the
end of the presen-
tation

Presentation Conferencing and Self-Running Presentations

Presentation conferencing enables you to run a slide show over a network or the Internet. To accomplish this, all participants must have PowerPoint 97, which includes the Presentation Conference Wizard. Choose Tools, Presentation Conference to start the wizard. (Figure 5.42 shows the first screen of the Presentation Conference Wizard.)

Some components of a presentation cannot be seen or heard by the audience during presentation conferencing, including embedded objects such as sound clips, video clips, and graphs. Sound effects applied to slide transitions and slide objects are heard only by those participants who have computers capable of multimedia.

The person presenting the slide show has access to tools, such as the Meeting Minder and Slide Navigator, and controls the show. Participants can use the annotation pen to write or draw on the slides, enabling other participants to see these annotations.

In PowerPoint 97, you can view a presentation on one computer tied to an overhead projector, while controlling the presentation with another computer. Use the Slide Show, View on Two Screens command to accomplish this. Each computer must have a COM port available so that they can be linked with a null-modem cable.

Self-running presentations are unattended presentations used at kiosks or booths frequently used at conferences, conventions, or trade shows. They can be interactive, where the user can select options to play multimedia components, branch presentations, and other hyperlinks. Self-running presentations are often set up to loop continuously. Additionally you can protect the self-running presentation from being changed by making most controls unavailable. Choose Slide Show, Set Up Show to select options for the self-running presentation. (Figure 5.43 shows the Set Up Show dialog box.)

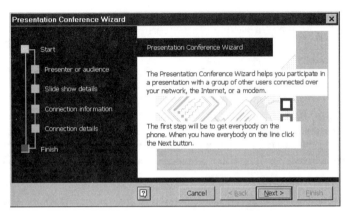

◀ **FIG. 5.42**
PowerPoint 97—
Presentation
Conference
Wizard

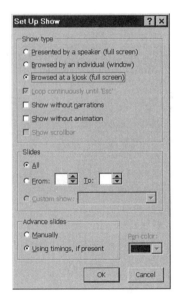

◀ **FIG. 5.43**
PowerPoint 97—
Set Up Show

Presentation Alternatives

Pack and Go Wizard and the PowerPoint Viewer

The Pack and Go Wizard was introduced in PowerPoint 95 as a means of compressing a presentation, making it easier to take presentations on business trips or sending them to others.

To access the Pack and Go Wizard, choose File, Pack and Go. The Pack and Go Wizard prompts you for information regarding which presentation to "pack." (Figure 5.44 shows the first step in the wizard—a road map.) The wizard can include the files to which you have created links (see Figure 5.45) and any embedded True Type fonts. You also are asked whether you want the PowerPoint Viewer to be included with the other files to be packed. (The final step is shown in Figure 5.46.)

The PowerPoint Viewer is a separate program used to run slide shows on computers that use Windows 95 or Windows NT but don't have PowerPoint installed. You can include the PowerPoint Viewer with the files in the Pack and Go Wizard or use it independent of the Pack and Go Wizard. When you reach your destination, run the setup file, **Vsetup.exe**, to install the Viewer program.

The PowerPoint Viewer program is located on the Office 97 CD under **Valupack/ppt4view**. Copy the **ppt4view** folder to a disk. Or, visit Microsoft's Web site to download the viewer.

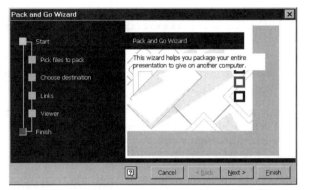

◀ **FIG. 5.44**
PowerPoint 97—
Pack and Go
Wizard

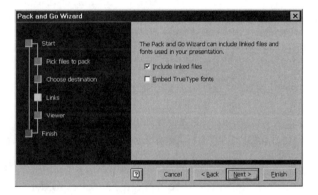

◀ **FIG. 5.45**
PowerPoint 97—
listing of packed
files

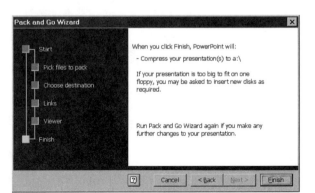

◀ **FIG. 5.46**
PowerPoint 97—
Final step

PowerPoint Presentations on Networks

If you have a company intranet or an Internet Web or FTP site, you can save presentations to these networks where others with similar access can view them. Use the File, Save As command to save your file to a network.

If you intend to publish a presentation on the Web, PowerPoint 97 includes several templates designed specifically for online presentations that can help you design a presentation for online viewing.

PowerPoint 97 comes with an Internet Assistant Wizard (see Figure 5.47) that quickly converts your presentation into a series of linked Web pages that are ready to publish on the Web. You can use the PowerPoint Animation Player to create dynamic, animated Web pages. You must use the Animation Player to see video clips in an online presentation. The Animation Player is an add-in program that works with your existing Web browser to play animated PowerPoint presentations over the Internet and in real time. Along with the Animation Player, you must have a browser and either Windows 95 or Windows NT to play presentations from the Web.

Choose Help, Microsoft on the Web, Product News for more information on installing and using the Animation Player.

Use File, Open to open presentations saved on your company's intranet or the Internet. A new toolbar, called Web, is available to make it easy to browse through presentations. (See Figure 5.48.) You can use the Web toolbar to open or search for Internet Web sites though your Web browser. The toolbar includes a **1** button to add interesting presentations on the Web to your Favorites folder.

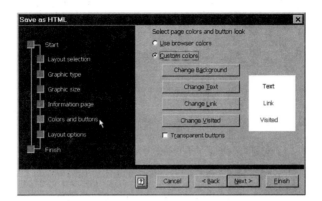

◄ FIG. 5.47
PowerPoint 97—
Internet Assistant
Wizard

◄ FIG. 5.48
Office 97 Web
toolbar

Index

190

self-running, 182-183
see also files; slide shows

Preset Animation command (Slide Show menu), PowerPoint, 160, 164

previewing
files, 2
presentations, 162

printing comments (Excel), 76

Publish to the Web Wizard (Access), 110-111

publishing slide shows on networks, 186-187

Q-R

queries (Access)
creating
in Design View, 124-125
with wizards, 122-123
editing, 126-127
Microsoft Query, 102-103

Query Wizard (Excel), 102

records, sorting/filtering (Access), 120-121

Records menu commands (Access), 120

Remove Filter/Sort command (Records menu), Access, 120

Report Wizard (Access), 128

reports (Access)
creating
in Design View, 130-131
with wizards, 128-129
formatting/editing, 132-133

reviewing document changes (Word), 52-53

Reviewing toolbar (Word), 48

revisions (Word)
merging documents, 50-51
reviewing changes, 52-53
tracking changes, 46-47

Revisions dialog box (Word), 46-47

rotating data (Excel 97), 68-69

rows in tables, distributing evenly (Word 97), 34-35

S

Save As dialog box
Access, 110-111, 146-147
new features, 6
Word, 40-41

Save As HTML command (File menu)
Access, 110-111
Excel, 64-65
PowerPoint, 156-157

Save As HTML dialog box (Word), 26-27

Save As/Export command (File menu), Access, 110-111, 146-147

Save In dialog box (Access), 146-147

Save Version dialog box (Word), 54-55

saving
document versions (Word 97), 54-55
files, 6
in HTML format, 26-27, 64-65, 110-111, 156-157
versions of, 21

searching for files, 4-5

Select Files to Merge Into Current Document dialog box
Excel, 99
Word, 50-51

select queries (Access), 124

self-running presentations, 182-183

Set Up Show dialog box (PowerPoint), 182-183

Shared Lists command (File menu), Excel, 94

sharing workbooks, 94-97

Simple Query Wizard (Access), 122-123

Slide Color Scheme command (Format menu), PowerPoint, 172-173

Slide Show menu commands (PowerPoint)
Action Buttons, 170
Action Settings, 166-169
Custom Animation, 160-161, 164-165
Preset Animation, 160, 164
Set Up Show, 182-183
View on Two Screens, 182
View Show, 162

slide shows (PowerPoint)
action buttons, 170-171
animation, 164-165
branches, 166-167
hyperlinks, 166-169
icons, inserting, 166-167
multimedia clips, 174-175
navigating, 162-163
Pack and Go Wizard, 184-185
PowerPoint Viewer, 184-185
presentation conferencing, 182-183
publishing on networks, 186-187
self-running presentations, 182-183
summary slides, 176-177

slides, expanding, 178-179

sorting tables (Access), 120-121

sounds in slide shows, 174-175

spell-checking (Word), 20, 28-29

Spelling and Grammar dialog box (Word), 28-29

Split Cells button, Tables and Borders toolbar (Word), 32

splitting databases, 108-109

STDEVA function (Excel 97), 80

STDEVPA function (Excel 97), 80

sum( ) function (Access), 142

summary slides in slide shows, 176-177